SECRETS *of* SUPER SALES PEOPLE

Why 80% Of Salespeople Fail
And How NOT To Be One Of Them

By
Debbie De Grote

D1445202

Anderson-Noble Publishing
Long Beach, California

Visit our Web site at **www.Excelleum.com** for more information on Debbie De Grote.

Library of Congress Control Number: 2014933177

ISBN: 978-0-9842827-8-4

Published in the United States of America by
Big Guns Marketing, LLC dba
Anderson – Noble Publishing
5150 E. Pacific Coast Hwy, Ste 200
Long Beach, CA 90804

Excelleum...When Excellence Matters

This book is available at quantity discounts for bulk purchases.
For information, please call 1-855-420-1400

This book is dedicated to Don, my husband, business partner, and best friend; who always believes in me even when sometimes I don't believe in myself.
Thank you for putting up with me!

About Debbie De Grote

Debbie takes great pride and joy in her work, which is also her life's passion.

Debbie's Accomplishments Include:

- 16 years in Real Estate sales; Hall of Fame Winner and Awarded Number 1 in Production in LA and Orange County for Century 21 International- 150+ sales/personal production in a calendar year
- Sales Office Manager for Century 21
- Corporate Recruiting
- Wrote strategic plans and launched new branch locations
- Vice President of Coaching for a large Real Estate coaching company
- Corporate Consulting
- Private Coaching, with over 52,000 calls completed
- Hired to train dozens of top real estate coaches
- Authored customized sales training programs for Real Estate and other industries
- Authored customized scripts for Real Estate and other industries
- Over 3,000 Group Conference Calls and over-the-phone training sessions

- 300 live training events
- Guest appearances on numerous panels and conferences
- Owner/President of Excelleum Coaching & Consulting®

Debbie has twin daughters in college. Taylor De Grote is a Business Major and desires to take part in the Company upon her graduation. After her degree, Erika De Grote will follow her parent's example and begin a career in real estate. She is a licensed agent. Debbie's loving husband Don De Grote is a successful Realtor and works out of Orange County and is the Chief Operating Officer of Excelleum®.

While the De Grote's call Southern California their home, they also enjoy spending time as a family at their cabin in Northern Idaho. When she's not working, Debbie spends her free time with her husband and daughters traveling. Debbie is also active in her local business community and is a member of the National Women's Council, and is on the Board of Directors of the California Association of Mortgage Professionals (CAMP), and is a member of First Christian Church in Huntington Beach.

In addition to her accomplished tenure in real estate sales, coaching and consulting, and starting her own firm, Debbie is also keynote speaker. If you're interested in arranging a speaking engagement, please contact her at debbiedegrote@gmail.com.

Table of Contents

Preface

I began my sales career quite by accident at the age of 18, while still in my senior year of high school. An acquaintance to my parents was a Real Estate Broker that needed assistance in their office. I was nearing that crucial time in my life where it was time to plan for college. Since my parents didn't have the funds to pay my college tuition, I decided to start selling real estate to put myself through school. My dream at the time was to buzz through college and go on to law school. I thought real estate would be a good way to fund my education. Once I started selling homes though, it was all over. I fell in love with it and never made it to college. What I chose for my career instead of bar exams, briefcases, and benches was to make "the art of selling" my life.

I started selling homes full time in the second semester of my senior year in high school when I would often close a transaction at an open house over the weekend. Because I was so young at the time, my broker advised me to dress older and lease a Cadillac Seville so that clients would assume I was successful and safe to work with. So I put on my cap and gown and drove my white Cadillac to my high school graduation, and the very next day jumped full time into my new career. By the time I was in my early 20's I was the *Number 1* agent in Production for Century 21 International in Los Angeles and Orange Counties, and *Top 10* in the world again for Century 21 International. I closed 150+ transactions in a single year at a time when the concept of teams was not yet popular.

I worked an insane amount of hours, took very few days off, but I was young and it was fun. However, the experience of giving up quality of life to hit the high numbers is one of the reasons I became a coach. My goal always is to help the salespeople I coach avoid the mistakes I made.

In my years of coaching I have put a lot of attention and energy into helping my clients build systems and teams to allow them to "have their cake and eat it too," to have a fantastic business and some life and time off as well.

Because of my success at a young age salespeople in the industry asking me to share my "secrets to success" often approached me. I found though that when I shared the truth about what I did, many found it was just too much work. However, some were excited and anxious to excel, they were special!

16 years ago I accepted a coaching position, coaching top real estate agents, teams, brokerages, and mortgage and title representatives. For 14 of the last 16 years I worked for two of the largest coaching corporations in the nation. While working for these companies I maintained a schedule of 70-80 coaching clients, many who were coaches in training. Each received a 30-minute call from me weekly at the same time, missing only a few weeks a year for holidays and vacations. I also would conduct on average 1-3 group coaching sessions per week with anywhere from 25-300 students on the line.

On top of this I would often hold webinars and breakout sessions, which were sprinkled in frequently throughout the month. I guess you can see that I am just as obsessed with coaching as I was with selling houses. The volume of coaching sessions and type of high level clients I deal with have caused me to become known as one of the most experienced coaches in the industry. I strive everyday to become better and to find new ways to help my clients, coaches, and myself keep growing. I tell my current coaches and all the coaches I have trained, we can never believe we are "good enough" we have to always get better, we have to always add more value, our clients deserve it. This I am obsessed with!

In April of 2013, it came time for me to start my own enterprise and I launched Excelleum Coaching & Consulting®, of which I am President and Founder. We coach salespeople and corporations of all types, sizes, and in a wide-range of industries.

As the owner of the company I have been able to bring all my years of selling and coaching experience to the table in creating a high quality company that really digs in to help our clients build a high quality business. I only hire coaches who have a tremendous depth of knowledge and business success and then I train them to be the best they can be at imparting their knowledge to our clients.

One of things about my company, Excelleum, that is different from most coaching companies is that we spend a full hour on each call with our clients. I found that while they needed and wanted accountability they also need us to help them create a blueprint for their success, which could include everything from hiring to managing money and profit to skill building and identifying market opportunities. That just couldn't be done in 30 minutes.

What is also different is that my coaches, including me, will not coach over 30 people, because we want to be very accessible to all of them in between calls. Many of my coaches are still active in the field and bring a straight-from-the-street approach, and even though I don't sell houses any more I spend several hours a week working with my husband on the family real estate business so I too am never far from the action. Additionally, our clients know that even when I am not coaching them personally I am still very involved. I know exactly what's going on in their business and I am always just an email or a phone call away. So in a sense they have two coaches working with them and the entire coaching team is on standby to help step in with their particular area of specialty when a client needs it. We feel honored that some of the best in the business choose us to coach them and are dedicated to doing our best.

I believe it's important to provide some insight into my background so that my readers can get a clear picture of the fact that if I could build a successful sales career, so can you! Like many of you I had no unfair advantages, no special talents or inside pipelines of leads- I had to build my business from scratch. I will admit though that I was determined, possessed a blind faith, and being as young as I was, I was fearless enough to believe that anything was possible.

One of the reasons I decided to write this book is because my daughter Erika is embarking on her own career in real estate. I wrote this to help her and decided to share it with you. In fact, as I am writing this she is dressed in one of my suits walking out the door to hold her first open house.

At the first sales meeting I ever attended I remember the broker had us chant a quote from Napoleon Hill, *"What the mind can conceive and believe it can achieve."* This broker is also the first person who ever made me write down a sales goal, and pressed me to think bigger. He gave me a copy of the book: *Think and Grow Rich* and told me to read it over and over again, which I did. This same broker also is the one who told me to dress older, lease a Cadillac, and learn my market inside and out. He knew that image and product knowledge was critical.

He also told me that since I was young and had basically zero skills I would have to prospect like crazy at least 5 hours a day calling, door knocking, and holding open house every Saturday and Sunday because my conversion initially would be very low. I suppose that since I was young and a student and used to being told what to do I just did it, and it worked.

I believe it was in my 4th year or so in the business when I broke 100 and then later went on to hit the 150+ mark.

How did I do it? Kind of simple actually, I never stopped prospecting 5 hours a day. What happened is that as my skills, knowledge, and client list grew so did my conversion. I was addicted to prospecting, because I knew no matter what I could always go find new business.

In my sixteen years in the trenches I experienced tough economic cycles. Yet I survived and prospered in spite of changing market conditions, competition, and rising interest rates- some of the things I bet you're struggling with right now. In fact, early in my career interest rates were over eighteen percent and I still sold houses! Because I never stopped prospecting! Over the years a few people have questioned if I really did the numbers I said I did, because they haven't personally been able to achieve them. However, I believe anyone could if they just PROSPECTED MORE!

In coaching sessions and in this book I never think that the way I did it is the only way to do it, I do not put my goals and standards on anyone else. I believe we all have unique gifts and we all march to the beat of our own drum. We all have different ways of measuring success. Whatever your goal might be you can do it! Many others before you have, many others out there are doing it right now. In fact, you will meet a few of them in the Hall of Fame section at the end of the book, be sure to read it, they are inspiring people.

A question I've asked myself, and which provided the basis for this book, is if a career in sales offers so much opportunity for economic prosperity, why then do so many people who are more educated, socially well connected, and probably much smarter than I am fail? I have attempted to provide some answers in this book and I have asked some experts in the industry to share their thoughts. Those are listed at the end of the book, read them and see which thoughts resonate with you.

As I wrote this book with my twenty-one year old daughter Erika in mind I also wrote it for my daughter Taylor, who is a business major, because even though she is not planning to be a salesperson I know that if she masters the skills outlined in this book when building her future business she will be a success.

With you and with them I would like to share the advice I've been given in my career, the "wins" and the "misses" I've either experienced personally, or observed in others, and to help all of you avoid some of the common mistakes that could derail your career.

This book is great for new sales people, but is also good for us veterans who know that we can always improve our game!

My years of experience have taught me that there aren't many, if any, "born salespeople." In my opinion anyone can be great if they are willing to do what it takes.

Are you willing to do what it takes?

I would love to hear from you and would very much appreciate your comments. Because I believe my clients and readers deserve the best, I answer all emails personally, so please feel free to reach out to me anytime at debbiedegrote@gmail.com.

My wish is that you enjoy reading this book as much as I did writing it, and treat it as a valuable resource for your prosperity. Furthermore, I hope that you will use it to its highest and best use, understanding that you are the master of your own destiny and you are in control of yourself and your business. It's your turn to EXCEL, and we are here to help you!

Best Wishes!

Debbie De Grote

President and Founder
Excelleum Coaching and Consulting®
Website: www.EXCELLEUM.com
2901 W. Pacific Coast Suite 200
Newport Beach, CA 92663
Toll Free: (855) 420-1400
Fax: (855) 559-9783

Chapter 1
The 1st Reason Most Salespeople Fail-
They Lack Heart, Passion, and Commitment

Is there such a thing as a "born salesperson?" Maybe, but I really don't think so. As I said in the introduction, I believe anyone can learn to be a great salesperson if they have the desire to be one. Sales is not an easy business and to succeed you need to have an unwavering belief in yourself and a relentless determination to get back up whenever the business knocks you down.

I still remember the first house I ever sold; I was 18, so excited until they backed out of the deal the very next day. I remember being a little tearful as I sat eating lunch with my dad, Norm at Taco Bell. He told me to knock it off and get back to work, that it wasn't going to be easy and I was going to have to fight for the success and be tough enough to take the defeats.

One of my favorite quotes is by the football coaching legend Vince Lombardi. He has so many- Google them- they are great to read and post. One of my favorites talks about the glory of lying broken and bleeding on the field of battle victorious. So yes, we all get beat up and feel beat up at times, but be tough get up and get back in the game.

After years of being immersed in the sales industry I have met many terrific salespeople and they come in all shapes and sizes. But what they do all have in common is their love of selling and their passion for the business. It takes courage and 100% commitment to wake up every day and make it happen!

I remember once being at a Sunday night dinner party where I declined the offer of a second cocktail, knowing that I had a busy day the next day. A friend at the party who was a salaried employee overhead me, and gladly accepted his third or fourth drink while saying "my boss gets what's left of me." I've never forgotten this and mention it now to convey to you that if you plan to not only survive but thrive in sales you can't do it with this type of attitude. Sales professionals who are consistent and productive know that every day we work is show time!

To achieve the stellar results you want for yourself you must show up everyday physically and mentally prepared to conquer.

A great salesperson's mindset is much like the mindset of a professional athlete; everything we do, everything we think, and everything we eat or drink will impact our performance. It takes discipline and determination to be consistently at the top of your game and quite frankly most people simply cannot maintain that level of discipline. (But my guess is those are the same people who have not purchased this book, so read on!) It's interesting to see this reality hit them in the first 90 days of their sales career- the reality of just how much work it's going to take to make it.

Once they realize just how hard they are going to have to work one of three things usually happens; they wash out right away, they step up their game and get on with things, or they choose to barely get by.

I'm curious… which one describes you?

Great salespeople never think things are "good enough." They are always on a quest for the next sale and the next level of mastery in their industry. Does this mean that they don't have dark days? Of course not! Top salespeople, *sales professionals*, realize when it's game time and they step it up and focus on the task at hand. They check their problems and their worries at the door and roll up their sleeves and get to work!

The top salespeople I know have mastered the discipline of doing the things others avoid doing and they do them at a high level. Their peers may even call them a machine because they approach the business in such a methodical and systematic way. Sure they may occasionally get lucky, but for the most part they leave very little to chance.

So what pulls them through the tough days? It's different for everyone, for some it's the excitement of achieving the goals they have set. For others it's the quest for financial freedom or security. Some love the recognition, rewards, and accolades. Whatever the hot button is that keeps them climbing the mountain, once they identify it what it is, it becomes the touchstone that helps them avoid complacency and keeps them on course.

I encourage you to take a few moments to answer the following questions:

What is your motivation?

What excites you about this business?

What keeps you going when the going gets tough?

How are you using this to motivate yourself and stay on course?

I want to reassure you that even the most passionate salespeople don't love their jobs every single day. What separates top achievers from the rest of the pack is that even on the days that they are downtrodden, deals fall apart, and personal problems and issues arise, they still prospect and they still do what they need to do. They've set goals, and just because their journey that day has provided some additional turbulence, they look at their goals, and understand that their bottom line doesn't change due to a bad day or week. They press on, they are fearless, they are determined, and they are unstoppable!

Let's go back to the professional athlete. Do you think they love practice? Do they love playing with an injury? Do they love the occasional losses? Of course they don't, but they love the game and they love winning and that keeps them going. We admire those who achieve greatness and yet sometimes fail to live up to the greatness within ourselves. If you want to achieve your goals you too have to embrace the thought that discipline is not an option. There is a price to pay for success and no one ever said it would be easy. Of course, since losing isn't much fun either then why not suffer a little pain to win?

While you will need to work hard to win don't suffer needlessly. Identify some of the things you really don't like to do, the things about the job that make you really unhappy, then by all means modify or eliminate them if you can.

Here's an exercise that might help you analyze what changes you could or should make.

Write down the 5 things you enjoy most about your job.

Next write down the 5 things you least enjoy.

Take a careful look at your list, are there ways you can spend more time doing the things you love? Are you maximizing the potential in your areas of strength? I suggest you post the list of the things you love and reread it on days you aren't feeling at the top of your game as a reminder of why you do what you do.

Next is a short list of some things that I love about being a salesperson:

- No one can put a ceiling on what I can accomplish.

- Every day I get to start over and make it happen.

- What I do is seldom boring.

- There is always something new to learn.

- I get paid well, far better than what I could earn if I settled for the proverbial notion of "security."

Email me and tell me what's on your list of things you love. I will put you in my next book. debbiedegrote@gmail.com

Next look at the 5 things you hate, and actually ask yourself why you hate them.

Can you eliminate or delegate any of them?

Do you simply need to work to improve your skills so that they won't be so difficult?

If you prospected more would they go away on their own?

If you improved your mindset would you hate them so much?

Since we mention mindset, let's be honest, sales success is mostly mental. Because staying at the top of our mental game is so critical most Top Producers have their own routines that they do daily to keep them on track toward their goals, just like a professional athlete has their rituals before a big game.

Below I've outlined a few favorites of Top Producers so that you can choose some that will work for you.

<u>Rituals & Routines of Top Producing Sales Professionals</u>

1) Read a good book- at least 15 minutes per day.

2) Listen to a motivational audio program.

3) Say affirmations throughout the day.

4) Belong to a Mastermind group.

5) Have written goals and review them daily.

6) Spend time inspiring people.

7) Exercise daily.

8) Have accountability partners.

9) Journal your wins and successes before turning out the light at night.

10) Never end your day with a negative meeting or phone call.

11) Attend training sessions and other motivational meetings.

12) Have a dream board with pictures of your goals.

13) Share your goals with those who believe in you.

14) Hire a coach!

Successful salespeople also understand that building their sales pipeline takes time and effort before they will see the fruits of their labor. They patiently and diligently work their plan with a blind faith that holds it's not a matter of *if* the success will come it's simply a matter of *when*. When you think about it, I'm sure you'll realize that any career that pays well will require a substantial investment of time and energy, so why would a career in sales be any different?

Chapter 2
The 2nd Reason Most Salespeople Fail-
They Don't Believe In What They Are Selling, Or Don't Believe
That What They Do Is Valuable

I remember my very first listing appointment with a very sweet Hispanic couple that I met at open house. They had a cute, clean property in a terrible, gang infested area. They were hoping to move into the area where they met me so that their children could play outside without the fear of being shot at and would have the kind of schools they deserved. It was their dream to make this move up for their family.

When I sat with them at the table they got scared, afraid to take the step, hesitant to sign the contract. I wasn't thinking about the commission I would earn as I pressed them to move forward, I was thinking about their goals and how it was the right thing for them. I had to convince them to do it!

Well they did it, and they happily moved to their new home and raised their children and sent them off to college. The last time I spoke to them their home was paid off and their piece of the "American Dream" was secure. In fact, the area they moved from was so bad that I couldn't sell their home. So I bought it from them and had my first rental, even though I was still living at home with my parents. Over the years I can't tell you how many times they thanked me for helping them make the decision. With them in mind I wrote this affirmation that is still on my wall today. "My job as a salesperson is to help people overcome their natural fear and hesitation to achieve the goal that they have set."

You notice I didn't force them to do something that's harmful, or that is not their dream to do!

I'd like you to ask yourself: what is your mindset toward salespeople?

When I'm asked by corporations to aide them in their selection of new salespeople there are a few questions that I always ask the candidates.

What experience, if any, do you have in sales, and what did you sell?

How did that go?

How do you feel about salespeople in general?

Were or are any of your friends or family in sales?

What did your parents think about salespeople?

No one in my family was a salesperson when I was growing up, however my father Norm was what you would call a "horse trader." He was always going to swap meets and garage sales, finding treasures, and selling them at a higher price. Years after I began my career he also got into real estate sales and built a very successful business working with my mom Wanda.

I have noticed that many of the salespeople that struggle do so because they grew up with a negative mindset about salespeople. I believe this is due in part to the fact that there are too many poorly trained, unethical, and unenthusiastic salespeople out there that give the good ones a bad name.

Vow to be different!

Vow to be better than average and vow to make a difference!

As I've gone through the years coaching and training sales professionals, I've noticed that many top producers were raised in households where the parents were in sales or at least were entrepreneurial. For those of you who grew up around sales it's far more likely that you see selling in a more positive light than those who did not. So a question I'd like you to ask yourself is: how have your personal beliefs impacted your mindset about being a sales professional? Is that mindset helping you or holding you back?

Since my daughters' birth they have been surrounded by salespeople. My husband is a very successful real estate agent in Southern California, and many of our friends and family members are in some type of sales business. If you asked my daughters what they think about salespeople they would probably say, "I think they are terrific- I want to be one!" While the fact that they have a positive mindset towards selling doesn't necessarily ensure they will be great salespeople, it does mean they come into the industry with better shot at it.

As we've established, most of your success stems from your attitude and mindset. Therefore, I cannot stress enough the fact that your attitude about being a salesperson is critical. If you don't believe in what you're selling maybe you should get a new career or switch to a new product. It's nearly impossible to be successful in what you do when you don't believe in it and in yourself. A salesperson said to me recently, "I believe in what I'm doing but I still have a negative mindset about selling and being a salesperson, am I doomed to fail?" My answer was no, of course not, however this individual has some work to do regarding their mindset. I shared with them a few suggestions that would help them improve their beliefs about selling.

Here is the list I provided them- perhaps it will help you too!

1) Interview as many great sales professionals as you can. Ask them to talk to you about the people they have helped and the grateful clients they have amassed. Then ask them why they feel what they do is worthwhile.

2) Make your own list of all of the ways you have positively impacted your customers.

3) Read biographies of great sales professionals whom you admire.

4) Work on your rapport building skills, the art of listening and the skill of asking great questions. When you can connect with people on a deeper level you will find you can zero right in and help them achieve their goals with very little effort. As a result, you will have better, longer lasting relationships with them.

5) Study the art of selling, and master your product knowledge. Being skilled in your profession affords you the time to focus on the needs of your clients. When you are good at what you do you don't need to be pushy.

6) Deliver outstanding service and ask your customers/clients for testimonials. Reread those testimonials often. This will help reinforce the belief that what you do is valuable.

7) Work with qualified and motivated people- they are more fun and you can convert them more easily.

8) Watch your negative self-talk. Even though we can't control the first negative thought that pops into our mind we can control the second.

9) Keep your goals in front of you, post them, review them daily and share them with those who support you.

10) Respect your clients, listen to them and guide them to take the steps they need to take. Suspend the thoughts of your commission and instead think about helping them achieve their goals.

I have a wonderful client Ernie Carswell, in Beverly Hills California. Ernie is Realtor to the rich and famous. He sells homes to Superstars, Hollywood A-Listers, and some of the world's most famous people (Katy Perry and Fergie are among those on his client list). Ernie and I recently appeared on a radio show in Newport Beach and during the interview something was said about how large Ernie's commission checks must be. Ernie shared with us that he never thinks about the commissions, in fact he never even knows what he has earned until his business manager tells him. He shared that he sincerely thinks only about his client and their needs. The rest will take care of itself.

As his coach I know that this is completely true. He is not only one of the best sales professionals I have ever met, he is one of the most kind and gracious people I know.

Many if not most of my corporate clients also share this philosophy. Battery Systems one of the largest independent distributors of batteries in the nation, and maintains a steady 97% retention of their customers. The owner, Brad Streelman encourages his team to exceed their customers' expectations whenever possible. While the company loves to earn new business, they put serving the existing customers first.

Another corporate client of mine, Stauber (a performance ingredients company), is also an independent company whose mantra is "amazing response time and over the top service." The list of incredible companies and sales professionals I coach who put client service first goes on and on. Even though many might ask: *why would individuals and companies who are already so successful hire my company to coach them?* It's important to note the answer: simply because they are never satisfied. They know they can always perform at a higher level and they also know that if they stop improving the competition will beat them.

I want to share with you a story about another great salesman. The late Charles Lane sold real estate in the Naples area of Long Beach, California. He sold multi-million dollar, waterfront homes and was a top volume producer. I met Charles in 1986 when my husband and I purchased a waterfront home he had listed. At the time Charles was in his early seventies and extremely well off. I remember asking him, "Why don't you retire? You could certainly afford to." He said, "Why would I do that? I love what I do!" He went on to share with me that he started his career in real estate at the age of sixty-one when he retired from a management position in the grocery business. He said that before he ventured into real estate he had decided on some ground rules for his life. He said, "For one thing, I will not work with people who are rude and do not respect me. I either enjoy them or I don't work with them." He said that he also did not change his schedule for anyone. He liked to meet his buddies for coffee in the morning and have dinner with his wife at 5pm. He also said that he did not respond to drama. He explained that if he got a call that something was urgent, he would give it two hours. He said that nothing in the business was a matter of life or death and often within the two hours things would work themselves out, and if they didn't then he would step in and fix them.

He was a dedicated salesperson and advisor to his clients and a pleasure to go through transactions with. I can't think of anyone who didn't like him. He loved his job, he enjoyed his clients, and he operated his business with the highest level of integrity. He was still actively listing and selling homes when he passed away in his mid-late eighties. I think of his words of wisdom often, I share them with many of the agents I coach.

If you don't have passion for what you do, maybe you need to take a look at how you do it. Maybe the way you are approaching it and the type of clients you're working with are bringing you down

Can you define who your "perfect" client is? Once you define them, then you can fine-tune your prospecting efforts so that you are spending your time on the kind of activity that will make you the most likely to find more of them.

What are the standards you set for the clients you're willing to work with? Make a list, post it, and measure the leads you have now and the new ones that will come once you outline your standards. If your clients are not a good fit for you or how you run your business, why are you working with them?

A few years ago I had the opportunity to moderate a speaker's panel of top producing real estate sales professionals- all selling well over one hundred homes annually. When I asked them to share one thing that they had learned throughout their career that was critical to their current business, they all shared a mutual perspective on the type of clients they should be working with. The consensus of these Top Producers was that the financial ability of a potential client to buy or sell with them didn't mean that they should always work with them. They talked about how some clients are high maintenance and low profit and by passing on them it freed them to work with clients they would enjoy and could convert more quickly.

Are you letting unmotivated or unqualified prospects rule your life and take advantage of you? If you are, I challenge you to think about how that is impacting your enjoyment of the business, and your quality of life.

Chances are, if you prospected more consistently you could weed out some of the less desirable prospects without anxiety because you would know that you have better ones on the way. As we close this chapter I want to encourage you to put a lot of thought into your beliefs about what you do, who you want to work with and what you're going to need to change to attract more of your "perfect" clients.

Chapter 3
The 3rd Reason Most Salespeople Fail-
They Lack Specific Goals Or If They Have Goals, They Lack A Strong Plan To Support Them

Whenever I meet a client for the very first coaching session the first thing I ask is what are your goals? The second thing I ask is how and why they chose those goals. Next I ask what their plan is to achieve them. As I ask these questions what I often find is that they don't have clear goals, or if they do, their financial aspirations are just arbitrary numbers they chose because they sounded good. So really it's just an idea, a wish or a hope but it's not a plan.

I also find that while they are often passionate about achieving their goals, there's a disconnect between the amount of time they perceive it will take them to accomplish what they've set out to do, and the amount of work it will take to make it happen. Sales is a numbers game, do you know what your numbers are or need to be?

As you set your goal ask yourself the following questions:

1) What is the sales quota I want to achieve?

2) What is the income goal I am looking to earn?

3) What are the specific actions I will have to take to get there?

4) What is the schedule I will need to support it?

5) What help do I need to get me there?

6) What skill/s do I need to master?

7) What financial investment do I need to make?

8) What is the price I am willing to pay?

9) What is the result if I don't achieve them?

10) What is the reward when I do?

I recommend you track your numbers and results very carefully for the first 90 days of the next selling cycle. At Excelleum we have a software system for doing so- please feel free to reach out and ask for help! As you track your numbers your personal ratios will begin to emerge. Once you know your actuals, you can adjust your action plan if needed to ensure you're hitting your targets.

Step one is setting a goal, step two is knowing the numbers you need to get there, and step three is having a clearly defined action plan.

Many salespeople have no idea how to construct an action plan. Instead of clear actions they will often list vague ideas.

Examples of vague ideas:

"I will work harder."
"I will prospect more."
"I will improve my skills."

Examples of clear action steps:

"I will get to work by 7:00 each day, Monday-Friday."

"I will prospect for 2 hours from 8:00-10:00, Monday-Friday."
"I will practice my scripts and objection handlers from 7:00-7:30 every day."

An action step is something so specific that a coach like myself can hold you accountable to it, and believe me when you hire us we will hold you accountable.

I've also found that while it's important to have an annual goal, most of my clients do better when they break it down to monthly and weekly goals with daily actions, kind of like eating an elephant one bite at a time.

When you achieve the goal, what will you do with the money?

Once my coaching clients have set their goals and have a clear plan to achieve them, I have them to do the next exercise- "Spend It On Paper."

I ask them to do the following:

1) Write down the business and personal cost of living expenses, including taxes- both monthly and annually.

2) Next I have them write down their income goal, subtracting their business and personal expenses and taxes. The result is the net profit they can expect.

3) After this I ask them to outline, on paper, what they would do with the extra money. I tell them to account for everything, listing exactly where the money will go.

The reason this exercise is extremely important is because most people lack motivation to stretch if they don't create a need for the extra money. We all live a pretty nice life so if we don't create a true need for the additional income, often complacency sets in before they will reach their goal. So by making a complete and detailed list of what you will do with the extra income you'll earn, you're creating a need for it. As you go through your year and review this list often, use it to fuel you to do what you need to do even on the days you don't feel like it.

Hungry salespeople usually accomplish more. And clients like to hire hungry, motivated, and enthusiastic salespeople because they feel we will be "all in" when working for them.

Remember the Napoleon Hills quote: *"what the mind can conceive and believe it can achieve."*

Another quote I like is by Earl Nightingale: *"you get what you think about most."*

When you have defined your plan, defined your goals, and are 100% focused on achieving them you will.

The more often you review them and share them with those who support you the more likely you will be to achieve them.

I read something interesting the other day; I read that crabs placed in a shallow bucket (that they could easily climb out of) will never actually get out, because as soon as one of them gets close to the top, the others pull the climbers back in.

The lesson here is that if you choose to share your goals with people who are negative and unmotivated their instinct will be to pull you down, right back into the bucket with them. We will talk more about this in a future chapter.

Find people who will be supportive and yet at the same time will be honest and willing to dish out a little tough love to keep you in line. Of course, you can hire us and we will be sure to push you out of the bucket!

Whenever myself or my coaches are working with clients to set their goals we are often asked, "shouldn't I set a really high goal?" This is my advice: it's wonderful to be a big thinker, and for some people setting super high goals is a good strategy. However, after 52,000+ coaching calls and sixteen years of coaching sales professionals, I find that for most of us, setting unrealistic stretch goals often has a negative effect. An unrealistic goal can cause you to give up before you even begin. I recommend that you set a goal that is attainable, and while it may not be easy to achieve you believe 100% that it is possible. Then if you hit the goal early in the week, month or year you can always have great fun setting a stretch goal! It's wonderful to be a big thinker, but we do need to sprinkle some reality into our plan.

Speaking of being a big thinker!

I'd like to talk about the importance of doing things that stretch the limits of your thinking. In 1981 I was twenty years old and fortunate enough to be in a mastermind group with some very successful veteran agents. None of the participants were actually millionaires, nor were we even close for that matter, we just all wanted to be. Our goal was to brainstorm and share ideas that would help us think bigger and think out of the box of what was "normal" in our industry.

When we met weekly we would discuss very specifically how we could build a career that would earn us $1,000,000 in commissions. This was back when the average commission was approximately $1,500. There might have been someone at that time in the real estate industry earning a million dollars but they would have been extremely rare, and I certainly didn't know of any. Of course earning a million dollars per year at this at that time in my life and career was an extremely lofty and unrealistic goal, but I was a big thinker. The discussions of how we would generate, manage, and grow our businesses served me well as I eventually went on to sell over 150 homes per year and began to earn the types of commissions we had dreamed would be possible. This group also taught me at an early age not to limit my thinking, not to believe that I could only achieve what the average sales professional in my market was earning. These mastermind sessions led me to do things that were at the time very unusual in my industry.

I was one of the first few agents to hire an assistant, hard to believe that this was so unusual when it's so common today. Even though no one else was doing it at the time- hiring support staff- I realized that if I wanted to go further, I was going to need to have help along the way.

Another brazen and cutting edge thing I did was to buy a cell phone. Don't laugh! It was cutting edge back in the day. In fact I was one of the first agents to have one. It was so unusual that a real estate magazine called and asked if they could interview me, and I became the cover story, the headline reading "Cell Phone- Tool or Toy?" Of course, it weighed about twenty pounds and I had to haul it around in a suitcase, and my phone bill was $1000.00 a month but I needed it. It wasn't a toy; it was a necessity.

Shortly after the magazine article appeared the President of Century 21 International called and asked if I would meet with a group of very wealthy Japanese businessmen who were interested in purchasing Century 21 franchises for Japan.

They wanted to meet this strange young girl who was selling so many homes to see if what I was doing could be duplicated in Japan. I have to say it was one of the most grueling meetings of my life. Through an interpreter they pounded me with questions for hours. They then left and implemented everything we discussed and sent me many, many gifts to thank me for my wonderful strategies. Little did they know I was just a kid willing to try anything new to succeed.

Times may change, but innovative, pioneering thought regardless of the day and age, will separate you from the pack.

To be certain you are blazing new trails and aren't stuck in the rut of doing what you have always done ask yourself the following questions:

"What great conversations am I having each week?"

"How am I challenging status quo, what is considered "normal" in my industry?"

"What new and out-of-the-box ideas and methods should I be implementing?"

"Should I be forming my own powerful mastermind group?"

I am not suggesting that you are always searching for a magic pill, one that will take the place of the hard work you need to do. What I am suggesting is always be looking for new and innovative ideas and possibilities, be willing to go outside of what everyone else is doing. Be different, be brave and be a big thinker.

"Help! I've fallen and I can't get up!"

If you're falling behind on achieving your goal, its time for a reality check. When salespeople tell me they are just not hitting their goals I always ask them this question: "Are you doing everything you can possibly do to achieve it?" Their answer is always "no." If you're like most and there are areas where you're not achieving your goals, it's reassuring to know that the goal is within reach if you simply turn up the activity.

It IS a numbers game!

So know your numbers. If you don't know your numbers how will you know if you are ahead or behind? How will you know where improvements need to be made?

As I mentioned we help our clients write their plans and have an electronic numbers tracker to help them chart their progress.

To begin your own tracking here is how you should begin.

1) Write down your goals- income and production.

2) Make a list of all of the key categories of the business you should be tracking.

3) Create a simple form or spread sheet or use our tracking system.

4) Log your numbers at the end of each day.

5) Review your numbers at the end of each week so that you can set new goals for the next week to make up areas where you fell short.

6) Review your numbers at the end of each month to check your progress towards your annual goal and make adjustments as needed.

7) Conduct a thorough quarterly review to measure where you are at, where you are falling short, and what specific areas

need more attention. Contact us we will give you a quarterly review form to make it easy!

Weekly Game Plan

Name:_____ Week of _____

	Goal	Actual
1. Days worked	_____	_____
2. Hours worked	_____	_____
3. Contacts	_____	_____
4. Total listing appointments	_____	_____
5. Total listings taken	_____	_____
6. Total listings sold	_____	_____
7. Buyer sales	_____	_____
8. Total price reductions	_____	_____

Projects and Homework

1.
2.
3.
4.
5.

Priority Action Plan

Project Name:

Action Item	Responsible Party	Due By	Notes

Project Name:

Action Item	Responsible Party	Due By	Notes

Project Name:

Action Item	Responsible Party	Due By	Notes

Project Name:			
Action Item	Responsible Party	Due By	Notes

Project Name:			
Action Item	Responsible Party	Due By	Notes

Chapter 4
The 4th Reason Most Salespeople Fail- They Hang Out With The Wrong Crowd

Are the people you spend your time with going to help or hinder your growth?

If you're hanging out with negative, small minded, small thinkers it will have an impact on you. They will drag you down just like the crabs in a bucket we talked about in the previous chapter.

Clients often ask me, "What do I do if I'm married to or related to a negative person?" Of course I don't suggest that you leave them, but I do suggest that if you find yourself in this situation, you gently nudge this person in a more positive direction whenever possible. Don't share goals with them if you feel they will try to discourage you. It might even be necessary to have an open, real conversation with them (in a kind and caring way) to share how their negativity is impacting you.

Isn't your positive mindset worth protecting?

As you choose your friends and associates, add some to the mix who are far more successful than you are. Spending time with people who have and do more than you do will often keep you from becoming complacent and will raise the ceiling on your expectations.

If you're hanging out with low achievers, ask yourself how this is impacting you and your future potential. We all tend to avoid things that make us uncomfortable. I know that reaching out to new people, especially those who are more successful than us, may seem difficult. But that's exactly why you should do it!

A useful analogy here is the children's toy silly putty. It's that stretchy clay that comes in a little plastic egg. If you take silly putty and stretch it and then release, it will rebound but when it rebounds it will not bounce back to it's original small shape. You, as a sales professional, are like silly putty. When you stretch yourself to step out of your comfort zone you grow, you develop, and you may find yourself inspired to think bigger and try even more new things.

I ask you to think right now of who in your circle you view as super successful and inspirational. This individual does not have to be in your own industry. I challenge you to call them, invite them to lunch or dinner, and get to know them.

Clean house- if there are negative associates or acquaintances in your life, consider spending less time with them or avoiding them all together. This was a concept that was hard for me to accept, especially since I began my career at such a young age many of the friends I had were not yet on my professional level. They wanted to go out partying and have fun, while I was diligently working to achieve my goals.

While I didn't judge their choices or their priorities, I resigned myself to the fact that while this was fine for them at the time, it just wasn't the path for me. I knew that I wanted more from life than being average and I knew that to achieve a level of excellence in my career there would be hard decisions and sacrifices I'd have to make along the way. I gradually came to realize that I had to detach myself from those who seemed intent on dragging me down. So by contrast I sought out mentors who could help me raise the bar on my skills and expectations.

Who are your mentors? Maybe it's time you found some! We have some great people in our coaching circle we would be happy to introduce you to.

Chapter 5
The 5th Reason Most Salespeople Fail-
They Don't Have A Schedule, And If They Do They Don't Follow It

I am always asked, "What was your schedule when you were selling so many homes?" Before I answer them I always ask, "Are you sure you really want to know? Will you believe what I tell you?"

Before I share it with you remember I am not suggesting that you copy it, I am simply sharing it in case you too were wondering.

5:00 Wake up and work out
7:00 At the office running expired listings and prepping
7:30 Calling expireds - I wanted to be the first one
8:00 Calling for sale by owners
8:30 Calling past clients, sphere of influence, and super hot leads
9:30 Cold calling neighborhoods
10:30-11:00 The rest of my lead follow up
11:00-12:00 Returning phone calls (remember there was no email) & meeting with my assistant.
12:00-1:00 Lunch, usually at my desk, as I prepped for evening appointments
1:00-2:30 Previewing properties
2:30-4:30 Door knocking
4:30 returning calls and meeting with assistant
5:30 Appointments or more prospecting until 7:00
7:00 Appointment
9:00 Sometimes late appointment in the busy years.

I remember one time a client called to list their home and I said, "I am sorry but I am fully booked for the next two weeks until 10:00 pm" and they said, "Oh that's okay. You can come at 10:00 tonight." I was so tired I wanted to cry. Again I ask myself why I didn't I think of having a team!

Saturday

8:00 At the office organizing and prepping
9:00 Return calls and lead follow up
10:00 Door knocking the farm or an appointment
12:00 Quick lunch then put up open house signs
1:00-5:00 Open house
5:00 On to my next appointment
6:30 Usually had an appointment

Sunday

Am Church
11:00 Appointment
1:00 Open house- the signs were still up from the day before
5:00 Appointment or home

My day off was Friday because I found it to be the least busy day of all and most clients didn't want to meet on Friday evening. I would usually take 1 week of vacation, normally around a holiday weekend so I wouldn't miss much of the action. I would take a few days at Thanksgiving and from December 20th until Jan 2nd off.

During the crazy years I had a few incredible assistants who I should mention. They worked tirelessly and handled huge volumes of work. Granted transactions back in the day were much easier to manage. There was less paperwork, no lengthy inspections, and no massive overload of emails. Still, I honestly don't know how they did it.

But they kicked "you know what!" They were amazing; I really need to recognize them. Bonnie Strunk Olson was the first of my best. She stood by me for years, put up with a lot, and then went on to become a very successful salesperson herself. Next in the stellar line up was Cindy Watry. Cindy was young, unlicensed, and possessed the most intense work ethic of just about anyone I have ever met. She was also with us for many years and went on to become one of the best escrow officers in the business. There were others who were good, but these two were with me in the peak years. They had my back and they managed everything they could to allow me to spend my time on income producing activities.

Choosing your right hand person is one of the most critical things you can do. When they are great they will free you up to be more efficient and to spend more of your time doing what you do best.

Gary Keller of Keller Williams says that "talent pushes." You need to hire people who will be "the wind beneath your wings."

I also need to mention that I had fantastic affiliates to whom I was completely loyal, and in exchange they went out of their way to help me. Having high quality affiliates that, in a sense, become an extension of your "team" will free you up to have more income producing hours in your day.

Last but not least I had a highly supportive broker, Gary Howard, who was a friend, mentor, and very tough accountability partner.

So I guess in a way I did have my "team." They just didn't assist me in selling and listing the houses.

I warned you that you might not like my schedule. However, remember that I also told you that you don't have to do it my way. I would ask you to think about your team, your affiliates, and your posse. What can you delegate to them that will give you more time to find new business?

Now that you have a clearer picture of my schedule and my posse you can see how I did the numbers that I did. It wasn't luck, it wasn't magic, it was just hard work and discipline. Anyone can do it if they take the actions they need to take.

You see, I realized that if I wanted to hit the monthly goal of selling and listing at least 12 properties per month I would need to keep up this pace or lower my goal. Eventually, a few years down the road, I did ease back on the throttle a bit as my husband later joined me in the business and we began to think about starting a family.

I remember during one of my peak years, possibly the year I was first awarded the number 1 for LA/OC for Century 21 International, my husband Don surprised me with a cruise he had booked for us. He wasn't in the real estate business at the time, was young, and just wanted to have fun. He hadn't realized that if I went on the cruise I would miss the critical crunch time of getting in those last few sales to hit the number I knew I needed to hit to win the ranking I wanted to win. He sadly cancelled the cruise but supported me in the goal, as he has always supported my efforts. It was worth it, I won.

Looking back, did winning the number 1 spot really matter all that much? Should I have gone on the cruise instead? Maybe, however that just wasn't the way I was wired. I was so focused and so close to achieving my goal I wasn't about to step out of the competition in the "last few minutes of the game."

That year my production numbers were so big that competitors I was running neck and neck with called for an audit. I happily cooperated with the team from Century 21 International who combed through each file to be sure it was legitimately my deal and that each had the full 3% commission per side. That was the rule back in the day. I passed the audit of course, and Century 21 International continued to audit my files and other top award winners each year, possibly still do so even today. This was something I always appreciated because it kept the competition clean, fair, and fun.

I remember one of my fiercest competitors and one of the people I admired most in the industry at the time, Vikki Morrison, called me after I won the ranking for Number 1 LA/OC and asked me to lunch. She asked me to share my secrets. I happily told her how I went about doing what I did. I will never forget what happened when told her. She just shook her head, held up her hand for the waiter and said, "I think after listening to that I need a glass of wine."

You see, Vikki had already achieved the rankings, she had more trophies than she knew what to do with, and was incredibly successful and at a different place in her career than I was.

That's exactly why when we coach our clients our goal is to first and foremost understand them and their vision for their life, not to just push them to cold call and hit big numbers. Remember, everyone's definition of success is different. What's yours?

What's really interesting about meeting new salespeople is that they often say the reason they got into sales is because they "wanted freedom." I've found that often that's a euphemism for "I just don't want to work very hard." Soon into their new sales venture most discover that having too much freedom gets them into trouble and they find that they aren't very good at being their own boss.

Scheduling and time management is probably the number one thing most of my coaching clients tell me that they struggle with. Considering all of the demands that pile on us daily I am not sure it's something we will ever fully master. Instead, I think of it as a "work in progress." I doubt if any of us were born disciplined. While it's true that your personality style or the environment that you were raised in has an effect, for the most part discipline is a habit that great salespeople have honed and developed over time.

I've talked about the importance of having a schedule that supports the goal that you've set. Now I'd like to invite you now to write down the income amount that you want to earn this year. Think about this as if you were hiring someone and paying them that amount of money- what would you expect of them?

Would you expect them to be on time to work?

Would you want them to limit personal calls, texts, and emails?

Would you think they should leave their personal problems at home?

Would you want them to dress professionally at all times?

Would you expect them to do what was necessary to get the job done with energy and enthusiasm?

So why don't you be what you would expect them to be?

If you acted everyday like the person you want to become how successful could you be?

Your ultimate goal should be that the majority (80%) of your day is spent on income-producing activities.

Most of the really great sales people I work with would admit that they fall into the 40-50% efficiency category, and yet they still make a lot of money. Imagine what could happen for you if you were operating at 80% efficiency!

A few years ago the pastor at my church asked the congregation to engage in an exercise; he asked us to imagine if we were given $86,400 dollars each day. The catch was though that you couldn't save any of it and you couldn't give it away. You had to spend 100% of it each day or lose it. He then went on to point out that the moral of the story was that we are each given 86,400 seconds each day and we can't save them up or give them away, once they're gone we can't get them back.

How effectively are you in spending your 86,400 seconds daily?

Do you regularly complete the most productive task at the most opportune moment? To clarify my pastor's intent- this doesn't mean that you have to be working all of the time. If it's Sunday afternoon and you are napping on the couch as you watch football it's possible that could be your most productive thing at that moment. Why I share the 86,400 second story is to illustrate that you must be strategic about when you do your activities and structure your schedule so that you are doing the right things at the right time.

I read that if Bill Gates was walking along and dropped a $1,000 on the sidewalk, it would cost him more money to stop and pick it up than it would to just leave it and keep walking. Crazy right?! Let's ask ourselves; why do some people accomplish so much more in their day than others? While it's true they could be smarter, and they could have some other advantages, often it simply comes down to how effective they are at time management.

Top salespeople are obsessed with their billable time; they work with a true sense of urgency. Often when we are driving on the freeway my husband, who hates to be stuck behind a slow driver, will comment, "They must not work on commission."

My VP of Operations, Gina, is a very outgoing and expressive person. One of the biggest challenges she faces while working with me is the fact that I am always looking at the clock timing our meetings and encouraging her to give me the bottom line. You see, I am extremely conscious of billable time!

To begin building an effective and efficient schedule that maximizes your billable time start by writing down your personal unbreakable commitments and obligations. Next write down your day/days off and your approximate starting and ending time for each day. Remember that your schedule needs to support your goal, so you must to be realistic about how much time you'll need to invest in achieving what you want to achieve each day. Next create, in writing, your perfect day. While it's not possible that everyday will be predictable, the more predictable your routine is the more likely you will be to have an efficient day or week. Additionally, once you establish a predictable routine and stick with that routine long enough, it will eventually become a habit. Once it becomes a habit you will find that you don't struggle as much to stick with it. It will become easier to show up and jump into action.

What Is The Best Time To Prospect?

"WHEN YOU DO IT!"

Most salespeople I coach though find that like I did the morning really is their best lead generating and lead follow up time. They are rested and fresh and feel it's the best strategy to get the tough calls out of the way. In fact, if your morning routine is efficient and productive the afternoon will usually flow nicely. So plan ahead for efficiency- it doesn't happen automatically. The perfect day really starts the night before.

Here are a few things to do to prepare for an efficient income-producing day:

1) Before you end your day, put away all files, return all calls and emails, and make a list of your top 5 key priorities for the next day.

2) Organize your call list or prospecting plan so that you are ready to roll first thing in the morning.

3) Watch what you eat and drink and get to bed on time.

4) Have a morning routine that gets you up and running; whether it's exercise, affirmations, spending 15 minutes with a great book, or practicing your scripts.

5) Try to avoid heavy administrative work or solving deal problems until your morning prospecting is finished.

6) Time block your activities throughout the day.

7) Give each activity 100% of your attention- multitasking is not a virtue in our business. It leads to mistakes and stress.

8) Be a clock-watcher and work with a sense of urgency.

9) Eliminate personal issues and distractions as much as possible. Let friends and family know your schedule and know when it's the best time to reach you.

10) At the end of each day review your day to measure your own performance.

I was watching a movie the other night and there were two attorneys in the scene, standing in a hallway talking about where they would go to lunch when suddenly one of them yelled out a client's name. The attorney he was speaking with asked, "Why did you just mention the client? We are only talking about lunch." The other attorney said, "If I mention his name then I can bill him for this conversation."

I'm certainly not bashing attorneys as I share this story, I'm simply making a point about how certain professions are very clear on logging and measuring billable time. By contrast in the sales industry, sales people sometimes forget to think about their billable hours. They often neglect to measure the income producing hours in their day.

Keep A Time Log To Measure Your Income Producing Time.

Here's an exercise that I ask my coaching clients to do. Buy a yellow legal pad and for two weeks jot down every single thing you do all day long. At the end of two weeks as you examine your time log you will most likely notice some patterns, some good and some bad. Once you identify the patterns that are inhibiting your efficiency you can then create actions steps that will help change the unproductive patterns.

As you're doing your time study take a look at these questions.

1) What am I doing out of routine or habit that is no longer profitable or productive?

2) Am I doing the most productive thing at the right time of day?

3) What am I saying yes to that I shouldn't be?

4) Who or what are the most common distractions?

5) What can I do about them?

My clients report that the simple fact that they are consciously keeping track of their time causes them to immediately increase efficiency even before their time study is complete.

Typically when new clients come to us for coaching, one of their biggest complaints is that they feel completely overwhelmed. One of the first things we do with them is have them take us through everything they have on their plate. I ask them to think about the circus performer who balances many plates spinning on sticks. Eventually the plates crash, so I ask them to eliminate as many of the spinning plates as they can.

Generally salespeople are influencers by nature and they tend to be very dynamic and exciting people. Often those around them nominate them for PTA president, head coach, committee treasurer, etc. Often when I ask if these activities are all things that are important to them and that they are highly committed to they say no. They tell me they just didn't know how to turn it down.

It's flattering to constantly be asked to be involved and lead, and we all want to be popular, but you must learn to say no. If it's not important to you and if it's not something you are really excited about doing then don't do it.

I tell my clients they can't fit 18 hours of activities into a 10-hour day no matter how efficient they are at managing their time. Something has to give! I ask them to eliminate anything they can to clear space for the things they need to and want to do. Next I ask them not to say yes to anything new in the future without thinking about it for 24 hours.

I've even written a script on this subject that I provide to them. I find that when they have someone else's words, the task of saying no is easier. A portion of it looks like this: "Thank you for thinking of me, but my plate currently is so full already that unfortunately I will need to say no." It might be a little uncomfortable to say no at first, and you might feel a little guilty. But it's probably the only way to achieve your goals and maintain some balance in your life.

Once you pare down your activities to what is truly important and necessary, put it all in your schedule- both business and personal commitments. Then, if it's not in your schedule, don't do it. You may find it helpful to share your schedule with your friends and family so that they can be supportive!

I suggest you use a large plastic wall calendar and mark your days off to attend seminars, vacations/holidays, and training events. If you have staff then you should color code your calendar and mark their time off too. Post your vacations first and make it clear to your staff that they cannot plan to be gone when you are. I also find it's helpful to see the year at a glance and to look forward to the days off. It's also extremely productive to set mini goals as you count down to your next getaway. Zig Ziglar once said, "If only we worked as hard every day as we do before a vacation."

One note of caution though- salespeople can get carried away when mapping out their schedule and overbook themselves. They sometimes create a schedule that is so unrealistic and tight that they cannot maintain it. When it's not realistic it will soon end up in a drawer or unopened on the computer. Understand that your schedule is a work in progress so if something isn't working, revise it!

If you stick with your routine by the end of a 90 day cycle you will find that it has become a habit and you will notice your stress is reduced, your days will be more productive, and you'll know where you need to be at every minute of the day. Commit to being 100% present in the moment- whether that's prospecting or enjoying your day off!

Chapter 6
The 6th Reason Most Salespeople Fail-
They Acquire a Basic Amount of Sales Skills, Then Stop Learning Once They're Just Good Enough to Get By

This is a perfect topic to follow our conversation about time management and scheduling because if your skills are incredible you will close a higher percentage of your customers and will do so with ease.

I am not a big sports fan, it's just not my thing, but I am a fan of athletes and the discipline it takes to be the best. I also love listening to the coaches talk about what they do to lead winning teams and how they help grow and develop the players.

I am sure you have read, like I have, that Vince Lombardi started each season by saying, "Gentlemen, this is a football."

Of course, these players had been playing for years and years, probably since they could walk. What I take away from this is that maybe the point he was trying to make is that you can't take anything for granted, you always have to go back to the foundation and find ways to improve. You can always do better and that maybe it's not about the new things you do but achieving greater mastery of the basics.

Last night my husband was watching someone interview Bill Belichik, head coach of the New England Patriots. He fascinates me because he is obsessed with what he does. He is possibly one of the best coaches ever in the history of football. He was talking about how challenging it is to coach Tom Brady, because he said in his frequent meetings and strategy sessions with Brady, Tom always comes prepared and always drills him for the next idea and the next winning plan. Sounds like they are a good match.

How hard are you working to perfect your skills?
How much time do you spend studying your product?
Where do you need to step up your game?

Take a moment to take the following skill evaluation. Score yourself on each topic listed on a scale of 1-10. A score of 10 is perfect.

Below each item I have given you some suggested action steps that may be appropriate to implement to raise your performance. After you score yourself you can choose from my menu of actions steps or create your own.

1) **Time Management - My Score Is:** _____

Suggested Action Steps To Improve:

a) Put a schedule in writing- post it and look at it daily.
b) Time block prospecting activities for the early morning.
c) Eliminate as many distractions as you can.
d) Eliminate any unnecessary commitments from your life as you can.
e) Time your activities and focus 100% on each as you complete them.
f) Share your schedule with staff and friends and family and ask them to support you.
g) Keep a time log for two weeks to help you identify time wasting patterns.
h) Measure your percentage of billable time at the end of each day.

2) Prospecting for New Business- My Score Is:_____

Suggested Action Steps To Improve:

a) Look at where your business is currently coming from- how can you extract more from that area?
b) Set a plan to have 5 different sources for new business.
c) Examine what opportunities exist that you're not currently tapping into.
d) Choose new activities that are a match for your personal skills/strengths.
e) Time block it and do it daily.
f) Have accountability partners to keep you on track.
g) Practice your scripts daily and have a pre prospecting routine.
h) Choose your numbers and organize your prospecting session the night before.

3) Presentation Skills- My Score Is:_____

Suggested Action Steps to Improve:

a) Upgrade and organize your materials and visual aids.
b) Have a powerful script and internalize it.
c) Prequalify every customer thoroughly.
d) Be extremely well prepared for each meeting- do your research carefully.
e) Know the competition and be prepared to demonstrate why the customer should choose you.
f) Identify your clients' personality styles and adapt to them.
g) Write down 3-5 key questions you want to ask them to launch your meeting.
h) Identify the top 3-5 objections you are likely to receive and be prepared to handle them.

i) Practice until you perfect it.
j) Record a live presentation if possible for later review and study.
k) Be prepared to close 5,6,7,8 times.
l) Evaluate yourself at the end –what did you do right? Wrong? What will you change the next time?

4) Phone Skills- My Score Is:_____

Suggested Action Steps To Improve:

a) Make more calls!
b) Practice scripts for 15-20 minutes per day.
c) Keep them in front of you, easily accessible.
d) Record your calls and replay them to fine tune areas of weakness.
e) Have a role-play partner.
f) Set clear goals before you begin to dial.
g) Mirror and match their rate of speech and tone.
h) Don't take a no when a yes is still possible.
i) Use tools to make the job easier, consider an auto dialer and a head set.

5) Handling Objections- My Score Is:_____

Suggested Action Steps:

a) Create an "objections handling" resource notebook- create a tab for each objection and collect and record great responses for each one.
b) Study your objections handlers for a few minutes each day.
c) Role-play them with a practice partner.
d) When a prospect gives you an objection follow this pattern; repeat back a bit of what they said, acknowledge them, ask a clarifying question, and then respond.

e) Stay calm. They have the right to ask what's on their mind, work to stay in rapport!

f) Handle it and then close again.

6) Asking Great Questions- My Score Is:_____

Suggested Action Steps to Improve:

a) Read and reread the book *The 7 Powers of Questions* by Dorothy Leeds.

b) Write down 3-5 quality questions to ask before each meeting or important conversation.

c) Stop talking so much, instead make it all about them.

d) Think carefully about where you want to lead them and then create the questions that will get you there.

e) Ask only one question at a time and let them answer before asking another.

f) Ask specific and open-ended questions if you want to get quality answers.

7) Sales Versatility & Building Rapport- My Score Is:_____

Suggested Action Steps To Improve:

a) Take the DISC test and learn about yourself.

b) Look for your clients' main style and work to communicate in the way they prefer to be sold to.

c) Mirror and match their rate of speech and tone.

d) Make eye contact.

e) Acknowledge and approve.

f) Ask more questions.

g) Put yourself in situations to meet new people and try new things each week.

h) Eliminate judgment and instead come from curiosity.

8) **Customer Service- My Score Is:**_____

Suggested Action Steps To Improve:

a) Ask your customer to define their service expectations.
b) Meet with your team and discuss a plan for how you will exceed their expectations.
c) Examine your current customer service practices. How should they be modified?
d) Read the book *Excellence In Service, The Nordstrom Way* and brainstorm how you can implement some of Nordstrom's sales strategies.
e) Conduct a customer satisfaction survey on each customer.
f) Look for common service complaints and fix them immediately.
g) Empower your team to make immediate decisions to solve customer problems- define clearly just how far they're allowed to go.

9) **Product Knowledge- My Score Is:**_____

Suggested Action Steps To Improve:

a) Make a list of the specific areas of product knowledge you need to improve upon.
b) Create an action plan for how you will go about it.
c) Add time in to your schedule for study.
d) Seek out experts who can help you and schedule time to meet with them.

10) **Goal Setting- My Score Is:**_____
Suggested Action Steps To Improve:

a) Do a complete analysis of your previous year's production.

b) Write down the goal you want to achieve.

c) Make a list of all current sources of business and how much business you plan to extract from each source in the coming year.

d) List all new opportunities you'll tap into and how much business they will potentially yield.

e) Measure the profit that will be achieved when you reach the goal and then spend that profit (appropriate it on paper) to create a realized need for it.

f) Revise your schedule to support your goals.

g) Share your schedule with those who are supportive of you.

11) Mindset- My Score Is: _____

Suggested Action Steps To Improve:

a) Review your goals daily.

b) Set aside time in your schedule for reading great books or listening to inspirational audio programs.

c) Eliminate any negative influences that you can- consider turning off the news.

d) Journal your wins each day.

e) Exercise. It produces endorphins, which triggers opiate receptors in the brain and is the body's way of giving you a natural high.

f) Try new things and implement new actions- it's hard to be depressed when you're busy doing good stuff.

g) Spend time with positive people.

h) Do one thing each day just for yourself.

i) Watch the negative self-talk. Tell yourself to "stop it." I know you can't control the first negative thought that pops into your head but you can control the second one.

j) Take care of yourself. Your mindset will be better when you are healthy.

12) Administrative Processes- My Score Is: _____

Suggested Action Steps To Improve:

a) Review your current systems. What are you doing out of routine or habit that is no longer profitable or necessary?

b) Hire the right people to help you. Pay a little more to hire good talent.

c) Have clear job descriptions and expectations for anyone on your team, including yourself.

d) Create a systems manual- outline every process and procedure for what you do.

e) Review all technology and internal support systems to be sure you are fully utilizing all benefits.

13) Managing Money- My Score Is:_____

Suggested Action Steps To Improve:

a) Do a thorough review of your current financial situation to determine your true financial state and monthly income.

b) Review your Profit and Loss and work to eliminate unnecessary spending. A good rule of thumb is: if it doesn't make you a profit, it doesn't stay.

c) Identify upcoming large expenses so you can prepare in advance for them.

d) Hire a great accountant (CPA) and possibly a financial advisor.

e) Visit your balance sheet each week so that you know at all times exactly where your budget is at.

f) Set a realistic budget and stick with it.

g) Think about large purchases for at least 24 hours before making them.

Now that you've identified the areas and activities that you need to work on to grow, be diligent in your efforts to master them. Schedule time to practice and study daily. You need to invest time working on your business, not just working in your business.

Additional Ideas To Grow Your Skills:

1) Have powerful scripts for everything you do.

2) Identify key objections and have 2-3 responses for each.

3) Study your competition.

4) Define how you will differentiate yourself from them.

5) Do ride alongs /shadow other top salespeople.

6) Read books that address the areas you need help in.

7) Listen to audio programs.

8) Have practice partners and regular practice sessions.

9) Record/video tape yourself in action or in role-play for your review.

10) Score yourself at the end of each presentation to find ways to improve.

11) Hire a coach.

How Did You Score Your Presentation Skills?

One of the most important skills sales professionals need to possess is their ability to be a powerful presenter. Many veteran sales people have not perfected their presentation and often are not powerful in handling the most common objections that they receive daily. Even if you are a great presenter if you aren't closing 97-100% of your sales you could still improve, right?

Is It More Important To Be A Great Closer Or A Great Presenter?

When I conduct sales trainings I always ask the group if they could pick only one to be good at, which would they choose? About 90% of the time they choose being a great closer. Interestingly, in reality it's actually far more important to be a great presenter. Think about it- when you do your research, prepare and deliver a stellar presentation, the close is often effortless.

I've made a list for you of a few things that every great presenter should know.

- The customer is always thinking, "So what's in it for me?" Be prepared to show them the benefits.

- Extensive research and preparation is critical- learn everything you can about your client, their needs, and your competition.

- Take the time to prepare an excellent proposal and a list of key questions to ask.

- Make sure your presentation is more persuasive than informative.

- Make sure your presentation grabs their attention.

- Practice your presentation.

- Make a list of potential objections and practice your best responses.

- Give yourself time before the presentation to get your head in the game.

- Bring your personality to the table, it's show time- don't be boring.

- Make the presentation interactive, don't pitch them or talk at them.

- Close as soon as you see the opportunity to do so.

How To Grab Their Attention:

The first eight seconds you have of a prospect's attention span are crucial. If you had only eight seconds to win or lose the sale, what would you say in those eight seconds to make an impact? What if you approached every presentation thinking, "What is the best use of the first eight seconds of this presentation?"

Here are a few ways that you can grab their attention:

- Tell a real life, third party story about something another customer has experienced.
- Give your prospect a critical piece of news or information that is relevant to them.
- Share statistics that they will find interesting.
- Give them sincere recognition or congratulate them on an achievement.

The Proper Use Of Visual Aids:

Sometimes salespeople use visual aids as a crutch, and often they completely overuse them. Based on the fact that 67% of people in the world are "visual learners" the use of visual aids can be helpful, yet they should only be used to enhance or highlight your presentation.

- Take only the key pieces you need, don't overwhelm your audience.

- Make sure your visual aids look visually appealing.

- Practice ahead of time exactly how you are going to use them.

- Don't immediately hand them to the customer, this will take their attention off of you. Wait and incorporate them into the body of your speech.

Now It's Time To Close:

Assuming that the customer is qualified and motivated and that you have just conducted an excellent presentation showing how you can solve their problems, now it's time to close. Often I find that even the best salespeople seldom go past three attempts to close the customer. For many customers you will need to close them five, or six, or seven, or even eight times. I have always taught that the first six no's are reflex and that you must first work past the reflex no's to close a prospect.

Here is an example of what I mean- I'm sure we've all gone into a department store on a mission to purchase a particular item, and maybe were even in a hurry. Once we've entered the store a very friendly salesperson probably asked, "Can I help you?" The natural response comes instantly and instinctively, "No I'm just looking" or "I'm fine thanks."

Wouldn't it make more sense to say, "Yes, I need some help. I'm looking for something particular." So why don't we do it?

I read an article recently that said that the average consumer today is hit with thousands (yes, thousands) more ad messages in the course of a single day than ever before. Think about an average day; watching the morning news on TV, billboard messages on the freeway, radio ads, magazine ads in your office lobby, branding on the coffee cup you drink from, reading the newspaper, and online ads while you check emails, Google directions, etc. (All these examples are just to name a few). In essence, this causes us to build up our defenses against being "sold." A great salesperson knows they have to get past the defenses and not take a no when a yes is still possible.

How do they do it? They keep probing, asking questions to find "the pain" and then they offer solutions and ask the customer to buy. If they meet resistance they dig in and ask more questions and try again.

You may ask- how many attempts to close can you make before you get stuck? My response to this is that I would like to challenge you in the next closing situation when you hit the no's, to go one step past your normal comfort zone and try to close them one more time. When that becomes your new comfort zone, stretch again and try to close them one more time. Do this until you can gracefully close them five, six, seven, or eight times. It does take practice and remember if you aren't practicing, someone somewhere is and when you compete with them, they will beat you.

Some Of My Favorite Closes:

1) The Assumptive Close. If you don't use any other close, use this one. With the assumptive close in everything you say or do you are acting as if they will say yes. You never say, "If you buy," instead you say, "When you buy." People like to be led so make it easy for them to go with the flow and move forward.

2) The Ben Franklin Close/Pros and Cons Close. When a prospect gets stuck, help them reason through it by taking a sheet of paper and writing Pros on one side and Cons on the other. As you create the Pros list gently help them along by adding additional pros to the list. When you get to the Cons

side of the column stop talking and let them struggle with it. Hopefully by the end of the exercise the choice will be clear.

3) Major Close on a Minor Issue. Quite simply, make a big deal of a small issue. Gain their agreement on the small point making it easy to move the forward on the bigger decision. For example: "When would you like to move in?"

4) Reduce it to the Ridiculous. Break down the cost that they are concerned with in such a way that is shows them how minimal any additional cost really is. Here is an example-let's say that I was selling you a home and the price you were going to need to pay was going to cost you an extra $50.00 per month. I could say this, "Mr. Customer for less than $1.66 per day you can have the home you love. When you think about it, it's less than the price of a Starbuck's latte.

5) Alternative Choice Close. In this close you are not asking if they will buy instead you are giving them options of how they will buy. For example: "Do you prefer to take possession on January first or fifteenth?"

6) Summary Close. This close works so well because you will help them with the decision by summarizing all of the benefits they will receive when they do.

7) Third Party Story Close. The brain loves to process information through stories, so third party stories have proven to be highly effective. It doesn't matter whether it's a story of something good or bad that a previous customer experienced, the point is that our current client would want to learn from it.

These are just a few, but they are my favorites because they are easy to use. Practice them because each closing situation will normally require more than one method.

Handling Objections:

In most presentations you'll receive some objections. If however, you notice you are repetitively receiving the same objection you'll want to examine your presentation. Ask yourself if something you're saying or doing is sparking the objection.

Throughout my career I've been told that an objection is simply a question in the mind of the prospect. While this may be true most of the time it could also be that they're just making conversation, venting the thoughts on the top of their head, or testing how hard you're willing to work to make the deal happen. Stay calm! When most salespeople get objections they lose control and get scared, then they start talking too much, they fidget and flinch and maybe even get a bit argumentative. Try to relax, work to maintain rapport, and probe to see how serious the objection really is and what the belief is behind the objection that's causing them to bring it up.

You don't always have to jump to answer every "objection" because again, they simply may be just venting thoughts. If it comes up again, especially when you are attempting to close them, then you need to handle it.

Ask clarifying questions to get to the heart of the objection and to be sure you clearly understand why they're asking it so that you can handle it appropriately. When you feel you have a clear understanding work to isolate the objection to be sure it's the only objection on the table. Whether you're prospecting, presenting or handling objections, work to stay in rapport. Persuasion does not occur easily when you do not have rapport

Become A Master At Building Rapport

Did you know that 50% of sales that are lost are lost because we simply didn't connect with the customer, or maybe we even repelled them? The secret to gaining rapport with anyone, instantly, is learning to adapt. Learn to be Chameleon-like! A truly incredible salesperson can connect with anyone, anytime, and anywhere. They close people naturally and easily.

Even if you feel that you're not a "natural" when it comes to meeting and greeting new people you can learn to be.

Here are a few basic principles to master:

1) Stop focusing so much on yourself.
2) Pay attention to them and make it all about them.
3) Be an active listener.
4) Mirror and match their rate of speech and body language.
5) Ask great questions, questions that gather information and spark their thinking.
6) Acknowledge and approve.
7) Be interested and be interesting.
8) Come from curiosity not judgment.
9) Pause in between important points and allow a slight pause after they answer you to show that you are listening.
10) Get comfortable with silence!
11) Put yourself in new situations that stretch you outside of your comfort zone.

People are like puzzles, and we are in the people business. We aren't trying to be mind readers or manipulators, instead we're simply looking to truly understand them and meet them where they're at.

Some pieces of the puzzle:

- How they dress
- How fast or slow they speak
- Their personality style
- The words and phrases they habitually use
- How much they smile
- How they make decisions
- Their values and beliefs

Be an active listener! Whenever I meet new salespeople and they tell me that they are "great talkers," I'm instantly concerned. Truly incredible salespeople are not great talkers, they're great observers and listeners. Stop talking so much! Especially about yourself!

It always amazes me how oblivious we can be about our impact on those around us. In sales, you must be self-aware. I was in a social situation recently where one of the people in the group dominated the conversation, going on and on about themselves, almost without taking a breath. They droned on about how smart they were, throwing out the titles of hyper-intellectual books they had read, the social connections they had, etc. This person also felt the need to toss in a lot of big words and phrases just to be sure their captive audience recognized their brilliance.

What was most interesting about this is that they didn't notice the group was completely alienated and each person was painfully awaiting our moment to escape their onslaught of self-involved words. I doubt that they have many friends and I wonder just how many sales they've lost because of their enormous need to exercise their ego. We all are guilty, to some extent, of the same thing though aren't we? If you want to be a better sales person, and want to improve the relationships in your life stop talking so much about yourself!

Google the YouTube video titled "The Me Monster" to watch a short comical clip that talks about the very strange human need to make things all about ourselves.

If you want to increase your sales and have them occur almost effortlessly then work on improving your overall communication skills and your understanding of personality styles. Commit to eliminating your annoying habits and commit to raising your charm quotient! Charisma cannot be underestimated in sales, keep working on your ability to build rapport. You will find that as your skills improve you will be able to easily persuade, motivate, and inspire people to take action.

Dealing With The Difficult Customer:

We are in a people business and people can be intimidating and challenging!

Improving your ability to manage tough customers and tough situations is critical to your success and will dramatically reduce the daily stress and increase your overall happiness in what you do.

- Step 1:   Determine what about this customer scares or intimidates you and think about what is your best strategy to win them over should be.

- Step 2: Walk a mile in their shoes, if they are angry or difficult remember we don't know what kind of pressures they may be under, gracious and look for a way to connect with them.

- Step 3: Always be the calm cool head, and keep your ego out of it. It's hard to do when you know that they are being unfair, remember the old saying- you can be right, or dead right. You may win the battle but lose the war, so you need to always allow them to save face.

- Step 4: Don't be defensive or argumentative, however, don't let them walk all over you either. Look for the most professional way to diffuse the situation, but do so with confidence. Look them in the eye and solve the problem.

- Step 5: Be a good listener and ask quality questions to get to the bottom of their frustration, find a way to connect with them. Be direct and ask them "what can we do to make this right?".

- Step 6: If a mistake has been made, apologize and make it right as quickly as possible.

- Step 7: Understand that sometimes no matter what you do some customers will always be difficult, just accept it, do the best you can and move on.

- Step 8: Work to leave each conversation on a positive note. Be clear about what action will be taken to resolve the situation and then be flawless in your follow up and follow through.

- Step 9: Don't avoid them just because they are difficult- it will only make things worse. Handle your tougher customers and challenges early in the day while you're at your best.

- Step 10: If you feel threatened, verbally abused or in danger in anyway talk to you the appropriate person for help.

Handling The High Maintenance Customer:

While the high maintenance customer isn't mean or angry, but rather needy and demanding- it's still draining your time and energy.

- Determine the value of the client- if you think they are too high maintenance and low profit, walk away.

- Clearly outline their expectations and create an agreement of how you will service the account and how often they will hear from you.

- Find ways to give them the attention they need, but control it the best you can. If they like to spend an hour on the phone with you, occasionally tell them at the beginning of the call that you have only X amount of time before you are expected on another call.

- Be proactive vs. reactive, if you reach out to them with the information they need at the times of day you are least likely to reach them, you may be able to get them what they need without a lot of unnecessary conversation. However don't overuse this method or you will have even greater issues.

- Don't add fuel to the fire- if they are excessive talkers who tend to ramble on and on keep the conversation on track, don't ask questions that will lead them down a rabbit hole.

- Don't add your own personal thoughts or stories to the mix, it will just take longer to close the sale.

- Look for ways to gently pull the conversation back on track.

- Master polite ways to interrupt them, call them by name, touch their arm, interrupt by acknowledging them or asking a question. Sincere acknowledgement goes a long way, sometimes they simply want your attention.

- Keep your commitments and make your communications as clear and direct as possible to avoid unnecessary drama and conversation.

- Know that at times you will just need to grin and bear it!

Chapter 7
The 7th Reason Most Salespeople Fail-
They Don't Ask Enough Questions!

As professional salespeople, our goal is to help solve our customer's problems and give them the level of service that they need, want, and deserve.

There is only one-way to truly do this well- ask a lot of questions.

When you ask quality questions a number of good things happen:

1) They feel special.
2) Your questions stimulate their thinking.
3) You gain valuable information.
4) You identify their pain and hot buttons.
5) They naturally open up to you more.

I recently read an article that stated that the average four year old asks three hundred questions a week and the average college student asks one. I can only speculate as to the reason why we grow out of asking questions. Perhaps it's because 95% of what we think about most is ourselves, so it makes sense that we lose our curiosity about others.

Because we cannot rely on our natural ability to ask powerful questions in selling situations, let's stack the deck in your favor. To ensure that you enter your next selling situation armed with quality questions take a few minutes before your meeting or call and write down 3-5 questions on an index card that would be appropriate for you to ask your customer. It will only take a minute to write them down and it will help you connect with your customer a lot more effectively than if you were to just go in and start your "pitch." As you adopt this practice you'll find that you no longer have to do so much heavy lifting and the whole interaction turns from a hard sell situation to a consultative conversation and an easy give and take of information. That allows you to smoothly and easily help guide the client where you need them to go.

As you write down your 3-5 questions ask yourself these important things:

1) Exactly what do I want to gain by asking these questions?
2) Who will I be asking the questions to?
3) How do I need to adapt my questions to fit with their personality style?
4) What do I hope to help them self discover?
5) What is the right time in the presentation to ask my questions?
6) Where am I hoping to lead them?

Question Do's and Don'ts:

Do feel free to ask questions you already know the answer to as long as it's not obvious to them and it will get you where you want to go.

Don't ask questions that are pointless, just for the sake of sounding concerned.

Do build as many quality questions into your presentation as possible.

Don't interrogate.

Do take notes of their responses.

Don't ask more than one question at a time.

Do allow a pause after they answer to show you're listening, and when they answer, give them physical and verbal acknowledgement as well as approval.

Physical Approval:

- Lean forward
- Maintain eye contact
- Nod head
- Take notes

Verbal Acknowledgement and Approval:

- Great
- Terrific
- You are correct
- I understand
- I can appreciate that
- Really
- That's interesting

When you need to ask a series of questions your speech can begin to sound like an interrogation. To avoid this you should sprinkle in a few question softeners, these will help your questions flow in a more conversational way.

Don't over use them, and mix them up so that they sound natural and not canned.

Question Softeners:

- May I ask
- Please tell me
- Tell me more
- What's important about that?
- I'm curious
- I was wondering

Not all questions are good! Be careful what you ask and think again about where you're trying to lead them. For example: "What do you like about X agent/competitor/salesperson?" The last thing we want to do is ask a question that will cause them to extol the virtues of a competitor.

Avoid Dead End Questions:

"Are you happy with your current salesperson?"

"Is there anything you need today?"

"Is there anything I can do for you?"

These are questions that are not going to help you gather quality information.

Vague questions won't elicit quality answers. Don't ask questions that are too vague. If you ask them something that confuses them or forces them to think too much, they'll shut down. Remember they have a lot more on their mind than the question you just asked them. The average person has up to seven things on their mind that they are thinking about at any given time. Understand that they're never completely riveted on you.

Make your questions as clear and specific as possible if you hope to gather quality information.

Question Types:

Assumptive Questions: these questions assume that the customer is moving forward with their decision and it's just a matter of working out details or timing.

"When would you like to close on the deal?"

"How much would you like to offer?"

"When would you like to begin?"

Assumptive Problem Questions: these are questions designed to turn up the client's pain and help them realize just how much they need you. Because of your research and knowledge of the client's situation you will know the problems they have or are likely to have. You can then construct your questions to direct their attention to the pain.

People won't usually make decisions or changes without pain, this is why it's so important to dig to find the pain, then dial up the pain to help them see the need to move forward and make a decision.

"How will you feel if another buyer gets your home?"

"What are some of the service problems you've had in the past with other salespeople?"

"What will happen if you don't make this decision today?"

Open Ended Questions: these are great for gathering information and sparking deeper conversations. Open-ended questions begin with who, what, where, when, why and how.

"What exactly were you looking to accomplish in this meeting?"

"How will you know when you have found the right home?"

"What are you looking for in a salesperson?"

Alternative Choice Questions: with this question type you're limiting the client's answer to one of the two choices you want them to make. It's a gentle way to move them toward a decision.

"Would you like to close on the home this month or next month?"

"Would you like to make the offer today or tomorrow?"

"Would you like to buy X or would you rather buy X?"

Clarifying Questions: one of the best question types. When a client asks you a question or gives you an objection, a clarifying question is a terrific way to buy you a bit of time to gather your thoughts and to dig in and make sure that you truly understand what exactly they're asking.

"Why is that important?"

"What would that do for you?"

"I'm curious, why do you ask?"

When you become a master of asking great questions you will be amazed at just how much people are willing to tell you.

Of course the magic will only happen when they sense that you have sincere and genuine interest in them and in what they are saying! You will have to work hard to improve your skill of asking great questions, and it will be an ongoing area for improvement throughout your career. Educate yourself on the subject and practice by writing out questions that you can ask for all of the customer scenarios and situations you encounter.

Be an active listener. Now that you'll be asking all of these terrific questions you'll want to truly listen to the answers. Listen with the intention of gaining understanding and insight into their emotions and into their thinking. Being a good listener requires hard work and patience. You have to slow down, calm down, and stop thinking about the commission. Just be in the moment with them, be completely focused on them, and show them that you care. Think about it like this- you and your customer are in a bubble and nothing else exists to distract you, you are completely engrossed with them.

Several years ago I had a chance to meet a very interesting man, he was a speech/charisma coach to many famous people and politicians. In fact, he coached Ronald Reagan while he was President on his delivery of speeches. This coach told me an interesting story. In the 1990s, during the time that Bill Clinton was President, he was invited to the White House for a private tour. This coach explained that at the time he did not personally think that Bill Clinton was a good President and he did not consider him a very moral man. He said that during his tour, a connection offered him the opportunity to meet the President. He thought, "even if I don't like him I should still meet him, after all he is the President."

He went on to describe his conversation with President Clinton by saying that in those brief moments he was mesmerized by him, and that he had never met anyone with so much personal charisma. He said that in that short conversation the President made him feel so special, asked him so many questions about himself, and he recalled that being in his presence felt like the world just vanished and it was just the two of them. He said from that day on, "I just couldn't help myself, I had to like him!"

What did President Clinton do that was so mesmerizing? He did everything we just finished learning in our last few pages. You can do it too- you just need to master the skill of charisma, and to do that, stop focusing on yourself and pay attention to others.

Chapter 8
The 8th Reason Most Salespeople Fail-
They Don't Spend Enough Time Prospecting New Business

Remember my old schedule I shared with you. My goal each day was to make at least 50 contacts. Back in the day when phone numbers were listed, no one had caller ID, and more people were home in the day so it was easier to reach them. Luckily there are many great tools and technologies now that we didn't have then. Use them. I think an auto dialer is a godsend. It allows you when doing your calls to quickly get to the people who are home. What ever tools you can utilize to make you more efficient and whatever changes you need to make to your environment so that it is more supportive of your efforts do it!

Set your daily prospecting goal, block it in your schedule, and stick with it.

Earlier I talked about how salespeople entering the business are often unrealistic about what it takes to be successful and hit their goals. I also explained that our sales businesses are numbers games and most salespeople don't put themselves in front of enough people each day to achieve the goals that they have set. Often they don't have a strategic approach to maximizing all of the possibilities in each of their sources.

Let's perform a quick analysis of your business. Take a minute and write down all of your key sources of business. Next list how many sales/gross revenue you generate from each of these sources on average weekly, monthly or annually.

Now make a list of everything you do to work each of these sources. Ask yourself, "Are you truly digging in deep and doing everything possible that you could do in order to maximize the potential business from that source?"

If you're like most salespeople you'll have to admit that you probably could be more efficient in how you work your key sources. When you think about it, this is really good news. Why? Because it means that there is untapped potential, so if you step up your game you can create additional sales and possibly without a lot of extra effort or expense. Next I want you to write down what 2-3 new things you must do for each source to fully extract all of the available potential business that there is to get.

Once you've strategized your plan for your current sources, you can move on to analyze what opportunities that your business or market is presenting that you're not taking advantage of.

Many of the salespeople I meet and coach initially come to me with only one or two sources of business. Perhaps you can relate. That's just fine if these sources are yielding the business and income you need. However, if you need more business then you need to find new sources to add and new ways to expand what you do. As you consider your potential new sources think about the cost involved in pursuing them, the potential benefit, the time that will be invested, and your level of personal commitment to the project. Once you've locked in on a new opportunity, create an action plan and a predictable system for working that source. Then master the skills, many of which have previously been outlined, that you'll need to conquer it.

Ask yourself, "What new sources or opportunities are you avoiding that you know if you just stopped resisting and pursued them, you would be even more successful?" Isn't the pain of avoiding it worse than the pain of just doing it?

I find that most salespeople need to spend at least 2-3 hours per day or more aggressively prospecting for new business. Yet shockingly many spend less than 30 minutes a day prospecting for new clients.

Why do they avoid what will get them paid? Below are the reasons they often give me:

- It's hard.
- I don't know who to call.
- I don't know what to say.
- I don't like to be rejected.
- I don't get enough results.
- I don't have time.
- It's boring.

Typically these are just excuses, the real truth is that they are avoiding prospecting because they have call reluctance.

Maybe they haven't mastered the art of handling rejection.

Maybe they haven't mastered the scripts.

Maybe they don't have answers for the common objections.

Maybe they haven't built a tolerance for dealing with the repetitious boredom of smiling and dialing.

Maybe they haven't time blocked it into their schedule and made it a standing appointment in their day.

Any of these sound familiar? If you embrace the fact that as a salesperson your number 1 job is to prospect, and do it daily, you'll find that not only will you get used to it, it'll become routine and you won't fear it so much. You don't have to love prospecting, just love what it creates for you. Keep your goals handy and review them often, it's your reason for powering through on the days you don't feel like it.

No one loves talking to strangers, so if you don't like it just know that there isn't anything wrong with that. Most sales professionals (even the top producers) all felt that way when we began. The only way to get over being rejected is simply to get rejected more! You will eventually build a tolerance for it. Practice makes perfect and eventually the rejections will roll off of you like water off a duck's back. It's just like going to the gym for the first time in months; you know how painful that can be. At first you think it will kill you and before you know it you actually kind of enjoy it! Or at least you enjoy the benefits when you get done.

I remember the first time my broker sent me out to door knock, I sat in the car and cried. Then when I finally got the courage to get out of the car I would just toss the scratch pad I was dropping off on the porch and run, hoping I wouldn't have to talk to them.

Next time I got a bit braver and I would actually knock, softly though, hoping that they wouldn't hear me. Finally, I got my fear under control and did it right, and guess what? It wasn't so bad!

You see, none of us love it. We just love what it creates for us.

Preparation is key!

Proper preparation will make it far more likely that you will have a successful prospecting session.

Plan your lead generation the night before. Plan out who you will call, then have your plan and numbers ready. This eliminates wasting time and energy getting ready to be productive in the morning.

Set aside time each morning before you begin prospecting to practice your scripts. Mastery of the scripts will boost your confidence and this activity is a great warm up for your day. Make a list of the 5-10 key objections you hear the most and have 2-3 responses for each. When you know that you're prepared with the answers to any objection you're much more likely to prospect because you know that there is nothing to fear.

Accountability partners are a terrific way to stay on track. I advise that you set one up for each day. If you're competitive like most salespeople, consider creating a contest or competition as a fun way to keep yourself inspired to prospect. Track and log your efforts and results so that you can determine your personal efficiency ratio. For example: How many calls do you need to make to set an appointment? How many appointments do you need to equal a sale? Etc.

Once you're aware of your efficiency ratio you can work to improve it and this ratio will let you know how to set more realistic goals and action plans. It will also help you fine tune and perfect your schedule.

It's okay to be a little anxious or fearful, those are normal pre-prospecting jitters. Just don't let them stop you. That's why most aggressive prospectors have a strong morning routine that includes exercise, practice, and review of their goals. All of this helps them get focused and ready to roll.

Carpe Diem – Seize The Day!

Prospecting Sources & Action Plan Worksheet

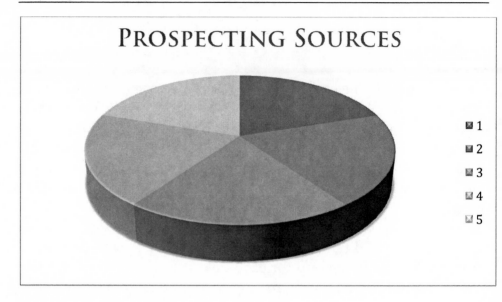

PROSPECTING SOURCES

- 1
- 2
- 3
- 4
- 5

Prospecting Activity:

Action Steps:

A.
B.
C.
D.
E.

Cost:
Expected Return:
Responsible Parties:
Major Challenge:
Solution To Challenge:

Chapter 9
The 9th Reason Most Salespeople Fail-
They Don't Work Hard Enough To Grow Their Database and Sphere of Influence

When you think about it, the sales business is really all about great connections. Some people are naturals when it comes to meeting, greeting, and building relationships with others.

One of the rewards that veteran sales professionals enjoy who have built and worked their databases efficiently is that the business comes to them. This didn't happen by accident.

Most salespeople never achieve this level in their business because they make a few huge mistakes:

1) They aren't effective in building relationships. This is either because they don't try or as I've previously stated, they need to improve their basic rapport building skills.

2) They don't treat their clients well and the clients don't want to come back or send them referrals.

3) They are unorganized and don't collect the data and enter it into a system that will remind them to consistently and efficiently follow up.

4) They might mail or email occasionally but it's not enough to keep them at the top of their client's mind.

5) They don't call their database contacts or attempt to connect personally so the relationships fade.

6) They aren't focused on new and creative ways to add new contacts to grow their database.

7) They don't have good scripts to ask for business.

8) They lack the right mindset about asking for business.

Are you guilty of any of these?

What would your business be like if you doubled and tripled your database over the course of the next year or two?

Can you imagine how much you would enjoy your job if you never had to cold prospect ever again? Well, do something about it! When you're more prosperous a year from now you'll be so glad that you did.

This is Your Database Action List:

1) Purge and clean up the list you already have.

2) Put your lists in an easy to use contact management system and carefully schedule your mailings, emails, and follow up calls so that they are automatic.

3) Comb through your cell phone contacts, checkbook, and credit card statements to determine who you know and who you do business with that are not on your list. Add them.

4) Create an "A List" of your top 25 contacts who will do more business with you or are a great source of referrals. Treat them like gold! Tell them how much you appreciate them

and how much you need their help in growing your business. If they love you, they will help you!

Set a plan for how often you will call your A List.

Make a B List that can be called less often but still need a plan.

Then make a C List that can also be managed by your team and possibly these contacts only receive an email drip or mail.

5) Determine your marketing campaign. Email drips are great, however a very small portion of your database will receive them or even read them. For your quality clients, a few touches a year by physical mail is best to ensure you stay on the top of their minds.

6) Set a sensible action plan for how often you should call them and provide them with value. On every call ask them for referrals.

7) Up your game in terms of your service. Your goal should be to create raving fans.

8) Say "thank you" a lot, and certainly at the close of the deal!

9) Look for opportunities to ask your contacts for referrals. When you've just delivered great news, or solved a major problem for them- those are the perfect times to ask!

10) If you have a newsletter or other valuable information that you send out, ask who they know that might also enjoy receiving it. When they give you new contact information

call the person, introduce yourself, and ask their permission to add them to your information loop.

11) Put yourself out there; network, watch for new businesses opening up in the area, and look for opportunities to be in front of large groups of people that can be good potential prospects for you.

12) Always add additional notes and client information to each client record. The more you know about them the more valuable the database becomes.

13) Find ways to make them feel special, send them birthday cards, holiday cards, and tokens of esteem. Connect them to others who could help them in their business. Refer to your notes when calling them so that you can focus the conversation on things that are important to them.

14) Keep it all about them, while they may want to know a little about you, but not much. What people think about 95% of the day is themselves so if you want them to love you, keep it all about them.

15) Keep your promises and commitments and don't promise things you can't deliver. We aren't perfect, yet you and your team should strive for perfection.

16) Say "thank you" a lot and show them you appreciate the business.

Chapter 10
The 10th Reason Most Salespeople Fail-
They Don't Invest Enough Time and Money In Themselves or In Building and Perfecting Their Business

It's interesting that most new business owners invest large sums of money to build and open a new business. In sales we often get a license (if one is required), go through a minimal amount of training, buy some business cards, and say "Here I am!" It never ceases to amaze me that salespeople don't approach their sales career with the same level of focus and commitment with which they went through high school, college, or vocational school.

Every business needs a plan. Every business needs financial reserves and a careful monitoring of the expenses and profits. Every business needs some sort of support staff in order to allow the proprietor to delegate low profit tasks.

To truly build a successful and viable business you will need systems and quality staff members. Once you have established your systems and processes you need to create a manual that documents and outlines each one of them. This ensures that you and your staff are all on the same page regarding policy and procedure, and this becomes an excellent tool when on-boarding a new staff member. The Procedure Manual should be used to train them and as a helpful reference tool for them to work from.

Often a great salesperson is not a great administrator- they are a "people person." They often fly by the seat of their pants and aren't adept at running their business like a real business. This leads to unnecessary stress and loss of clients due to mistakes or gaps in service.

When hiring someone to help you with the administrative side of your business, don't hire yourself (someone with your same skill set). Instead hire someone who possesses the skills you lack. Then outline a clear job description for them and be clear on the priorities and deadlines of the projects you assign.

Work hard to be a good boss, staff turnover is a huge drain on time and resources. Pay more for quality people and then hold them to high standards. If they are excellent at what they do the returns will be tremendous.

To Begin Improving Your Efficiency, Ask Yourself These Questions:

1) What systems need improvement immediately?
2) What am I doing out of routine or habit that is no longer profitable or necessary?
3) How can I better manage my emails and social media channels?
4) What can I delegate that I'm holding onto?
5) What training or direction does my staff need in order to be more efficient?
6) Am I clear in my instructions?
7) Do I meet with them often?
8) How am I inspecting what I delegate?
9) Am I inspiring to work with?
10) Do I have the right people on board with me?
11) Am I a good boss?

Now that you've answered these questions you will most likely have a list of areas that you can improve on. Remember what I discussed earlier- changes don't usually happen unless you have an action plan to make them happen. So outline 3-5 action steps to improve upon any of your areas of weakness as a business owner. Set time lines and then get in action!

How To Be A Great Boss A Quick Review

1) Hire the right people.
2) Clearly define the expectations.
3) Be a great example.
4) Communicate with them.
5) Listen to them and encourage them.
6) Be realistic in your expectations.
7) Invest time and money to train them.
8) Confront at the moment when needed, don't harbor grudges.
9) Be clear on your priorities and deadlines.
10) Ask for their input and opinion.
11) Respect their personal time and life.
12) Set goals and hold them accountable.
13) Avoid criticism and when you must criticize, do so in private and also acknowledge what they do well.
14) Reward them for peak performance.
15) Thank them for their support.

Four Key Areas of Focus To End With:

As we wrap up or conversation, I wanted to leave you with four key areas of focus.

1) Take care of your existing customers- new business is wonderful and necessary, however it's a lot harder to win new customers than it is to keep those that you already have. Commit to raising the bar on your communication skills and levels of service and always look to exceed their expectations in every way possible.

2) Get the right people on your team! Look at your staff and support team, are you utilizing them to their fullest potential? Are you clearly communicating your needs and expectations and are you delegating everything you can delegate?

3) Stop being a "secret salesperson" and find low key ways to let everyone you meet know what you do, then add them to your database. Get yourself out there by networking and meeting and greeting more business people. Ask the individuals you already know and currently do business with to help you meet and network with the people they know. This business is all about great connections- make some!

4) Manage your time effectively- it is your most precious commodity so don't waste it. Work with a sense of urgency and add more billable time/income producing activities to your day. Then go home and have a wonderful life.

Epilogue

As you read and worked through this book I'm certain you found areas where you can improve. Most likely they're areas you already knew needed improvement. Maybe you've tried to improve upon them in the past, yet didn't have the proper support and failed.

Changing our habits and pushing ourselves to grow is not comfortable. In fact, most people will do anything they can to avoid it. But you're not like most people are you? Even when we want to change it's not always easy to see the flaws in ourselves. It's not always easy to push ourselves and this is exactly why most successful people have coaches.

Think about this; an athlete could run the same play over and over again without any real improvement if they don't have a coach to tell them just exactly what they need to do improve. Coaching is not an expense; it's a tax-deductible, valuable, educational investment in yourself and your future. You can't afford not to do it!

Ask yourself if you're ready and if you're coachable. Being coachable doesn't mean you're looking to be micro-managed. It simply means you're open and ready to take your profitability to the next level by receiving some help and guidance to achieve all of the goals you've set. Furthermore, to be coachable you need to have an open mind. You must give up thinking you "know it all." Finally, you need to be willing to step out of your normal box and begin to push past your fear and hesitation daily to achieve the goals that you have set!

You'll have to be willing to admit that you need help, and then you need to seek the right kind of help. When you hire a coach that you trust you can feel confident that they have your best interests at heart. A great coach will be able to see clearly where you're at, be able to look ahead to where you can be, and help close the gap to get you there.

So, how do you find the right coach?

1) Look for someone you can respect because they have the integrity and background that gives you the confidence that they know their craft and know how to help you.

2) Look at their track record and level of experience.

3) Ask questions to inquire how they will customize their coaching for you personally. They should be tailoring your discussions to your needs.

4) Interview them; don't be afraid to ask them direct questions.

5) Ask for references from current clients.

6) Don't try to look good, tell them the truth about your weaknesses and fears.

7) Be prepared for your coaching sessions, take notes, complete the actions and reach out for help when you need it!

Call Us Today! We would be happy to put you in touch with one of our coaches for a complimentary coaching call to discuss your coaching needs and the goals you have for your business. Also feel free to email me with any questions you may have. We work as hard as you do and we are always ready to help!

FREE GIFT: To thank you for reading this book and as a way to help you jump start your career I would like to offer you my 80+ page Real Estate Script Book and audio download. You can obtain it by visiting the website powerpersuasionscripts.com.

If you need scripts for mortgage, title insurance or home/life insurance email me. I have those too! debbiedegrote@gmail.com

Before you put this book down to go sell something take a minute to review the coaching and training programs we can offer you. Choose one you are interested in and call us. We are here to help!

To Your Success!

Debbie De Grote
President and Founder
Excelleum Coaching & Consulting®
Website: www.EXCELLEUM.com
2901 W. Pacific Coast Suite 200
Newport Beach, CA 92663
Toll Free: (855) 420-1400

Thoughts From Industry Experts

A few of my favorite people have volunteered to share their thoughts on "Why 80% of Salespeople Fail And How NOT To Be One of Them."

I hope you enjoy what they have written and I appreciate them and thank them for taking the time to contribute.

Daryl Owen, CEO
Nationwide Real Estate Executives
Buena Park, CA

A career in sales offers the incredible opportunity to literally write your own paycheck. Yet most salespeople never tap into their true potential particularly, in my opinion, due to the fact that we sometimes lose grasp or focus of our direction. When confronted by the freedom real estate sales offers, we generally lack the self-discipline to be in the office every day, and stick to a strict schedule. The lack of consistency, persistency, and drive contributes to 99% of all failures in sales. Find your purpose, and what drives you. This will help you weather the storm and persevere.

Dan Stauber, CEO
Stauber Ingredients for Innovation

Dear Debbie,

When I think of those who have failed, those who have survived, and those who have "thrived" as a sales person with our company, I would break it down via a few key descriptions or observations.

Virtually every hire is "personable" and "relationship oriented," they wouldn't dare venture into sales if they weren't. The short lived "failures" typically find that they don't have the drive, nor the stomach for the constant "pleasing" it takes, nor the constant rejection. They don't invest enough time or energy into understanding it is a marathon, not a sprint.

Those who last a little bit longer, in my opinion, are the "coy" ones, the "hiders." They talk a big game, say the right things, constantly harp on past experiences or contacts (who they know), constantly surround themselves with a flurry of activity, but they are avoiding reality. After a series of months of lagging activity, or in some cases where they are lucky enough to be in a territory that is busy despite their "individual effort," (thank our Sales Support Department and/or Business Development for that sales activity) they can't explain why sales are what they are. Well, the "hiders" and the "coy" get exposed.

These first two types usually exhibit these behaviors fairly early on, but sales people as you know are tricky by nature. I have been burned before, held out longer than I should have on someone, "thinking and hoping" that our initial instinct about them could become true. I have gotten better about trusting my gut, cutting losses sooner, moving on.

The "survivors" are the ones who have a good balance between drive, work ethic, overall people skills, and "enjoyment" in what they do. They will always have a place in a good company, as long as the company pays the right attention to them, takes care of them, and keeps them engaged.

The "THRIVERS" have all of the traits of survivors, but at a much higher level. Not only are they self-starters and highly motivated, but they are overly ambitious & competitive, yet appreciative of the goal of the TEAM. They "want" to help achieve the goals of the company. They take pride in the building, and are not always concerned with "selfish" goals or objectives. They are able to "step aside from themselves," work together, all for the greater good. I love THRIVERS. That is who I want to surround myself with, and I am extremely fortunate to have a stable full of THRIVERS. My responsibility is to help them grow, put the right tools in their hands, keep them motivated. Compensation happens along the way. My suggestion would be "Find and fill your company with THRIVERS!"

Stay Positive+

Brad Streelman, Owner and President
Battery Systems Inc.
Garden Grove, CA

Great salespeople all have a game plan. They never wake up in the morning and say, "What will I do today? Who will I see?" They have a plan and strategy all mapped out and ready to go. If you don't have a plan then the first phone call or distraction that comes along knocks you off your game. When you get up and aggressively work your plan you will have some wins and some losses. That's business, and at the end of each day you evaluate that day and set your new plan for tomorrow. I recommend to my sales team that at the end of their day they ask themselves, "What did I do right? What did I do wrong? What will I change tomorrow?"

A great salesperson also has flexibility, which allows them to be prepared to handle the obstacles that are thrown at them each day. When I was playing football my coach would tell me, "You have to be multiple." He explained that what he meant was that I had to be able to adjust quickly to something that came at me outside of the window of my game plan. In business you may think you have the competition figured out and then bam! They blind-side you. If you don't have the skill set and mindset to dust yourself off and adjust your plan you won't survive and you certainly won't thrive. Great salespeople never think they are good enough; they are always working on their skill set because they know that if they don't somewhere someone else is practicing and could beat them. Great salespeople are super competitive, super focused, and driven to win. They push themselves to the limit each day; they push themselves way beyond their comfort zone. It's all part of what makes business and sales so exciting.

There are no limits except those you put on yourself. Quite simply, you have to want it and you have to be willing to fight to get it!

You stay hungry.

Mark Prather, CEO
Mark 1 Mortgage
Cerritos, CA
Phone: (714) 752-5718
Email: mprather@m1m.com

The Art of Selling!

Why do so few do well in sales? There are many reasons why people fail at sales. In my experience the number one reason is the belief system of the individual. The negative thoughts that they have about selling and/or about themselves positions them psychologically so that when they encounter the first bit of adversity they give up. Why do people have a negative association with sales? It may be because of the pushy sales people they have encountered through their lives or the bad jokes about used car salesmen. Or they may have a negative association of what selling is.

Selling is also about what you believe about yourself. Do you believe you are loaded with charisma and a real people person or do you shake in your boots at the idea of trying to sell someone something? Early in my career I asked myself these questions. I realized my problem with selling was that I believed selling was the art of manipulating someone to buy something they didn't necessarily need or want. This was something I wasn't willing to do, so I then had to ask myself the question if I wasn't willing to do this then what was I willing to do? Was selling the right career for me?

In thinking about this it occurred to me the truth is we buy things because we want and/or need them. So I realized what I had to do was start by finding people that wanted and/or needed to buy my product. I then realized if I focused on serving their needs by finding out exactly what they were looking for and why I could then fulfill those needs thereby making a sale without trying to sell but instead serve them! I believe that is what good salespeople do fill needs.

By going through this analytical process I had completely changed my belief system about sales.

The best part of your beliefs is that they are yours and that you have control of what you believe. However, changing what you believe is not so easy; it took years for you to become you. So if you don't think you are Mr. Charisma that can sell anyone anything and wonder if you can develop the confidence the answer is yes. Confidence comes from skill development. Selling is a combination of art and science. The art is your ability to connect with people. The key to connecting with people is to be more interested in them than yourself. If all of your thoughts are about you then it will be difficult to connect with your customer.

Hall of Fame Interviews

Over the years I have had the pleasure of meeting and working with so many great salespeople.

In the next few pages you will have a chance to get to know a few of them.

I selected them because not only are their results outstanding, but their ethics, their integrity, and their commitment to those they work for and work with are over the top.

They are gracious, they are humble, and I feel honored to know them.

Enjoy!

Jill Pursell
Georgetown, Texas
Phone: (303) 324-2874
Email: jill@pursellrealtygroup.com

Jill transferred her background in Business Administration to the Real Estate Industry in 1996. After initially building a successful business in Utah, Jill's family relocated to several different states due to her husband's work, thusly Jill's experience in building a profitable Real Estate business from scratch is unparalleled.

Debbie: **What is your secret to success?**

Jill: I have always had a coach that has held me accountable and encouraged me towards success.

Debbie: **How did you choose a career in sales?**

Jill: I started out as support and quickly realized that the guys I was working for didn't have anything special that I didn't have except that they were getting the big bucks!

Debbie: **What is the one thing you feel new salespeople joining the industry should know before diving in?**

Jill: You need a good support group around you and it is not a get rich quick type of career. If you work hard you will build and become the successful sales person you wish to be but it will not happen overnight. It's about consistency.

Debbie: **Knowing what you know now if you were starting over today what would you do differently?**

Jill: Not beat myself up and feel like a failure if I didn't reach my goal initially. It is a goal...something to strive toward, and realize that it is the journey that gives you the real enjoyment...not just the end result. Enjoy life more! Work will always be there.

Debbie: **What is your greatest strength and how does that help you?**

Jill: My greatest strength is being able to understand what my clients are going through and help make that process, which is highly emotional, as easy as humanly possible.

Debbie: **What do you observe as the biggest mistake that most salespeople make?**

Jill: Not setting realistic goals or not writing their goals down, and then not having the support around them of people who care about them and will hold them accountable and want them to succeed.

Chris Egan
Huntington Beach, CA
Phone: (714) 403-6824
Email: chris@chrisegan.com

Chris began his real estate career in 1981 at the age of 23 as a Mortgage Broker at *Mark 1 Mortgage*. Due to his top performance, passion for his work, and tenacious business sense, Mr. Egan took part in building *Mark 1 Mortgage* into one of the largest Mortgage Brokerage companies in Los Angeles and Orange Counties.

Debbie: **What is your secret to success?**

Chris: The secret to my success is being persistent in my follow up and consistent with my sales and marketing efforts. I recall early in my career, when real estate offices were open to sales calls from loan officers, that I would make my calls until I was able to get a lead. I had the mindset at that time that I would not go home until I made a solid contact with a new Realtor and obtained a good buyer lead from that agent.

Debbie: **How did you choose a career in sales?**

Chris: I did not choose a career in sales on purpose, I just happened to stumble into it. Back in 1981 a friend from high school who had just opened a mortgage company approached me and offered me a position as a loan officer with his company. I was not trained in sales or in real estate and I did not even know what a mortgage was. But I realized that without a college degree, sales would be the best way for me to make a decent living. I basically decided at that time that I would do everything I could to be successful in the mortgage business and make this my life long career.

Debbie: **What is the one thing you feel new salespeople joining industry should know before diving in?**

Chris: The biggest downfall that I have seen with sales people in my career is that they are not organized and they do not have a plan for success. I can remember that a Realtor would give me a lead to follow up on and then they would have to call me back to get the prospects number because they did not know where they put it. This is an example of not being organized and not having a plan for success. Most sales people do not have defined goals or a business plan. I believe that to succeed in sales or any business for that matter, you need to have a plan for success and this is where most people fail. Sales is a wonderful and rewarding field for those who will fully embrace it as a career. It is rewarding in the fact that you are able to help people fill a need and you will get paid very well if you are successful in helping others get what they need. Zig Zigler once said, "You can have everything in life you want, if you will just help other people get what they want."

Debbie: **Knowing what you know now if you were starting over today what would you do differently?**

Chris: If I were starting my career today, I would become more of a student of the sales and marketing process. I would commit to investing 10% of my income into a marketing plan and I would also purchase every book, tape, and seminar on sales and marketing that I could afford. I have learned from my own personal experience that it's not what you know that counts; it's who you know. Meaning no one cares how much I know about the loan process if they don't know that I am even in the loan business. You need to get your message out to the marketplace and that is where your success will come from.

Debbie: **What is your greatest strength and how does that help you?**

Chris: I believe that my greatest strength is being organized and persistent with my follow-up and follow through with my clients and my referral partners. When we choose a career in sales we are in a relational business. People who like you will do business with you. So you need to be likeable and be able to develop a personal relationship with the people you expect to do business with. This does not mean to be fake and phony with people because people can tell if you are a fake. You have to be authentic or people will see right through you.

Debbie: **What do you observe as the biggest mistake that most salespeople make?**

Chris: The biggest mistake I see in most salespeople is not taking the business serious enough and treating it like a career rather than just a part-time job. It's fairly easy to get a real estate license so I believe that leads people to believe that it will also be easy to put a few deals together. As you know that is very far from the truth. The reality is that real estate sales or sales in general can be very lucrative for those who are willing to put the time in to learn about sales and marketing, to put together a business plan, and to work the plan until they are successful. Most people will stop and give up before they reach the finish line.

That reminds me of the story called "Three Feet from Gold" found in the book *Think and Grow Rich* by Napoleon Hill. You will have to read the book to get the whole story but it takes place back in the gold rush days when the author describes a story of a person who was drilling for gold in Colorado and was making a fortune from his claim when the vein suddenly became dry. They drilled desperately in an attempt to pick up the vein but to no avail. The decision was finally made to quit, sell the equipment to a junk man, and return home with their claim and resume their life as it was.

The story goes on to say that the junk man sought out the advice of an expert in the field of mining for gold. This mining engineer examined the mine and calculated that the vein would begin just three feet from where the previous owners had stopped drilling. This is exactly where the gold was found. The moral of the story is that you will experience some defeat along the way, but with some expert advice (coaching) you can turn these minor setbacks into success.

Michele Safford
Northville, MI
Phone: (248) 912-8929
Email: michele@michelesafford.com

Michele is a licensed realtor who has greater than twenty-one years of experience in the real estate industry. In addition to her real estate license, Michele holds a Master's degree from Oakland University and a Bachelor's degree from Michigan State University, both in Special Education.

Debbie: **Michele, you and I have known each other for quite some time. You have been a consistent top producer for that entire time. How do you do it?**

Michele: I try to stay connected with my past clients minimally on a quarterly basis. Phone is the best but if that is not possible mail out something quarterly. Our team sends out quarterly newsletters.

Debbie: **How many transactions do you personally average per year?**

Michele: I personally do 50 - 75 transactions per year.

Debbie: **Where does most of your business come from?**

Michele: Most of my business comes from past clients and having built a reputation within the local market with consistent sales.

Debbie: **I know you have a very successful small team but these transactions do not include them correct?**

Michele: Together the team closes 85 - 100 per year, including my transactions. This year 55 were my transactions and 30 from leads I generated for the team.

Debbie: **What is the goal for your team this year?**

Michele: Our team goal for this year is 125 transactions.

Debbie: **Can you share with the readers how you consistently hit the big numbers?**

Michele: We consistently hit the numbers of our goal by maintaining a high level of personal client care service when we work with a client. We never take for granted that we don't have competition on an appointment even with a repeat or past client. You have to earn your client's business each and every time. It should be easier on repeat transactions but you cannot take it for granted.

Debbie: **What are you doing to make sure that you stay at the top of your game and to stay a step ahead of your competitors?**

Michele: I stay ahead of the competition with excellent communication and lead follow up. Too many agents work hard to get the listing but don't deliver outstanding client care service before, during, and after the sale.

Debbie: **If you could only pick 1 of your qualities that is your** biggest strength what would that be?

Michele: My one quality that is my biggest strength is working daily on being a better listener. It is not about me it is all about the client. Really listen to what your clients needs and expectations are. If you really listen intently they will tell you.

Debbie: **If you could give one piece of advice to the agents reading this what would you say to them?**

Michele: Begin each day with Gratitude, which will lead to wealth and incredible opportunities to have any lifestyle you desire.

Monica Reynolds
San Diego, CA
Phone: (760) 632-8408
Email: monica@hellerthehomeseller.com

Monica is a partner with Chris Heller and is the general manager and listing agent of the Keller Williams Real Estate Group in San Diego, California. In 2013, Monica and the Heller team closed 209 homes, at $98.7 million dollars in closed volume.

Debbie: **You and I have known each other for a long time. I believe when we first met you were one of the partners in a team in Long Beach and we were friendly competitors.**

Then we met again years later when we both came to work at the same coaching company and became great friends.

If my memory serves me right you were a super successful agent in Fargo, North Dakota prior to your success in Long Beach weren't you?

Monica: Yes, I started my career in Fargo, North Dakota. The first year I was Rookie of The Year and ultimately became the Top Agent in Production in the MLS before I moved to California.

Debbie: **How many transactions did you personally do in Fargo per year?**

Monica: Before I relocated to California in the late 80's I was doing over 175 homes per year with one assistant.

Debbie: **Again, these were your own transactions without the help of buyer/or listing agents?**

Monica: These were all my transactions...I did not have a buyer agent. I had one assistant.

Debbie: **How did you do it?**

Monica: I was a prospector for 2 hours a day. I was a great networker, Girl Scout leader, Junior League, and I worked with 2 top builders and had their business exclusively.

I also believed in asking for referrals from everyone. I had a system to get more than one transaction out of every client.

This was the day before computers so my index cards were my 'future transactions.' I called those every day. If it snowed and school was closed...great day! Everyone was home, and I called the phone book. I had what I called a snow file and I could easily set 2-3 appointments per day or more when it snowed.

I also door knocked for specific listings for a specific buyer. I loved the challenge of finding the home 'off market.'

Debbie: **How much did you prospect?**

Monica: 2 hours per day, and at the time I prospected all the new doctors coming to town, the list was available, and all the new birth announcements. In the 80's it was announced in the paper.

I was a 'digger' and most agents just waited for the business in my market.

Debbie: **What was your schedule like?**

Monica: I dropped my kids off at school or the bus at 7 am. I was at my desk by 7:15 and starting my calls.

Debbie: **You were a single mom for most of your career correct?**

Monica: Yes, I was a single mom most of my career.

Debbie: **How did you balance career and family?**

Monica: I had a very precise schedule that my kids could count on so I did not get too guilty. I never had an appointment between 3:30 and 5:30. That was my time to pick up the kids from school and do after school activities.

On Tuesday and Thursday I had a sitter come in and help with the kids and I would do evening appointments those 2 days only. Again, I had a schedule. My family also knew I was available Saturday morning and Sunday morning for family stuff. Saturday afternoon and Sunday afternoon I could be gone on appointments.

When cell phones showed up I did not bring it into my house. I had the 'kids' rule. When I came into the home, I became Mom, not Realtor Mom.

Debbie: **I remember you once told me that you told the kids they could have one of the 3 D's for dinner; deliver, drive through or don't do it!**

Monica: That is true...not sure how proud of that I am.

Debbie: **You and I are kind of a like, both maniacs when it comes to business! I know why I am such a maniac, what drives you?**

Monica: I love the Real Estate game! I love competition. I follow other agent's stats in my market place, what they list, sell, etc. When I see a listing in my 'area' from a competitor my first question is 'How did I miss that? What am I not doing? Why didn't they list with me?!'

I also love helping people with the American Dream of buying and selling real estate.

Real Estate is so fascinating and it affords women a 'no ceiling' job. Nationally women earn 77 cents compared to a man who earns $1.00 for the same job. Real Estate is definitely a place where women are paid on performance.

I love being the best I can be and have always strived for excellence.

I love learning and love applying it to real estate. I love buying property and investing. It is the only thing to invest in for the future in my opinion.

If you hold onto real estate you always win. I was always driven to provide my family with everything possible. I never wanted to say, 'No, we can't do that.' I always had great goals focused on providing the best possible life for my children.

Debbie: **We have both been challenged over the years by people saying the big numbers we achieved both in sales and coaching simply couldn't have been possible.**

Monica: As a disciplined person I accomplish a lot. I have a very precise/time blocked schedule. I have rarely deviated it from it.

Obviously, common sense, sometimes I reschedule but I always do what is important first, and if I miss that I go back and accomplish it before the end of the day.

I get up early and follow my schedule. Currently, the afternoon is time for appointments. My listing appointments are 1:30, 3:30, and 5:30. I don't deviate much from that. I control my schedule and agenda not the client. In 2013 my team and I closed 209 transactions and sold 98.7 M in volume. We had a great year and we can do more this year.

Debbie: **What would you like to say to the doubters that would also encourage the up and comers in the business?**

Monica: If you are goal oriented and a hard worker this is absolutely an amazing career with no limits on income or opportunity. You have to be a self-starter and focused. You must be disciplined and willing to learn every day. If I described you then you will be a successful agent.

So to the naysayers: this job is definitely not for you.... did I say also you need to be a positive person?

Debbie: **I know that you are still actively selling and running one of the most successful teams in the nation. For those who want to build a team or have a team and want to run it more efficiently what advice would you give them?**

Monica: The key to a building a team is to have 3 focuses:

1. Hire correctly for the job. Hire the right person. Have a detailed job description and schedule and make sure your hire is the best possible candidate for the job. Make sure the person you hire sees the opportunity you offer and is excited to be part of the goal. Hire Talent! Hire Talent! Hire Talent!

2. Systems are critical to duplicating and growing the business. All your checklists and systems have to be scalable and duplicable to build the business. You can start today by manualizing what you are doing and making each system better continually. Besides all the customer service systems you will need a precise lead generation system. What are the sources of your business? What is your plan to implement and increase business with these sources? Be very clear about your sources of business and you need at least 5 lead generation sources of business.

3. Create a realistic business plan and hire a coach. Create a business plan with an organization chart and future organization chart. The first hire is an excellent assistant with great computer skills, communication skills, and attitude.
The next hire is a buyer agent. Have a business plan for this year and also set one for year 2, year 3, year 4, and year 5. Make sure you have a step-by-step process and it is realistic.

This is how you build a team: right hires, systems, and a realistic step-by-step business plan. The last key ingredient for building a team of course, hire a coach. A coach will take you out of the learning curve and also save you money in costly mistakes.

Nick Roshdieh
Newport Beach, CA
Phone: (949) 254-4779
Email: nroshdieh@homgroup.com

Debbie: **What attracted you to real estate?**

Nick: The fact that I had the ability to run my own business and grow with a pace that best fit my personality. Being my own boss and controlling my own destiny.

Debbie: **Why do you feel you have been so successful when so many others have failed?**

Nick: I've always had good coaches who guided me in the business so I did not have to re-invent the wheel. Also, I took my job very seriously and treated it like a professional. I read books and met with many good agents to seek knowledge and guidance. I also worked extremely hard and efficiently to grow my business. Often people get complacent when they do not have someone to answer to but I did the opposite. At the end of the day I would give myself a score sheet of how I performed that day.

Debbie: **What is unique about you, the services you bring to your clients, how you attract business?**

Nick: I believe that we are in the service industry and it means a lot when a client hires me over many other good agents, so I give my client AAA plus service. I go over and beyond the client's expectations so that they would never forget how good the experience they had with me was. This results in a tremendous amount of referrals that continue today.

Debbie: **If you were entering the business today what would you do differently?**

Nick: I would interview and join a team with a proven track record for the first two years so that I would learn the business from a top producer.

Debbie: **What would be your advice to new agents that would help them succeed?**

Nick: The business is a marathon and not a sprint. Have six months of reserves saved up so that you are not in a rush to get your first sale.

Debbie: **What do you love about what you do?**

Nick: I love negotiating transactions for my clients. It is an honor to represent people's largest investments and I absolutely love leading the way for them and creating a win-win for all parties involved.

Debbie: **What are some of your biggest challenges?**

Nick: I believe that our biggest challenge is always self-doubt. We all have it. I work on it through prayer and usually shut that voice off most of time.

Debbie: **What is your goal for the year 2014?**

Nick: To continue on the path of balance which for me is God, Family, and then work. This way I can be my highest self for everyone.

Ernie Carswell
Beverly Hills, CA
Phone: (310) 988-9255
Email: ernie@carswellcollection.com

Ernie's real estate career began in the exclusive Highland Park neighborhood of Dallas, Texas. In the 1980s he moved to New York, gaining new perspective as an agent on Manhattan's Upper East Side. He moved to California in 1990 and has been here ever since, representing an extensive roster of satisfied clients including Fortune 500 CEOS, professional entertainers, top studio executives, attorneys, government officials, ambassadors and foreign dignitaries.

Debbie: **What attracted you to real estate?**

Ernie: Quite frankly, the people. In the beginning, not the people of the population as clients or customers, but the people of real estate themselves. I walked into a Dallas Texas residential sales office back in the early 80's and witnessed what appeared to be happy people, talking freely among themselves and a certain liveliness within the office atmosphere. This was incredibly attractive to me! Of course, later I learned it was all due to the charismatic office manager Mary, who was an influential person in my career from day one.

Debbie: **Why do you feel you have been so successful?**

Ernie: Because I gave myself no alternative but to succeed.

Debbie: **What is unique about you?**

Ernie: I approach each client as someone who needs me and my expertise and offer up myself with complete trust- until that trust is broken. Basically, I believe in the good of people until proven otherwise.

Debbie: **If you were entering the business today...?**

Ernie: I would only begin in today's real estate world as an apprentice under a successful, reputable leading agent. There is so much to be learned, and things are moving extremely fast in the technology world —which didn't exist when I began. That's why it makes complete sense to learn under the watchful eye of someone successfully navigating today's real estate market, in any town or city.

Debbie: **What would be your advice?**

Ernie: Give of yourself freely and the money will follow in due time.

Debbie: **What do you love about what you do?**

Ernie: Just about everything except the paperwork!

Debbie: **What are some of your biggest challenges?**

Ernie: Keeping pace with technology to keep an edge. Of course, for veterans, it's important to remember our experience is the Ultimate Edge!

Debbie: What is your goal for 2014?

Ernie: To follow my coach (Debbie De Grote's) guidance more dutifully so I can grow my business.

Marty Rodriguez
Glendora, CA
Phone: (626) 914-6637
Email: mr@c21martyrodriguez.com

Marty and I met sitting next to each other at Century 21 conventions. We were both top award winners and working like mad women. Marty, after all these years, still maintains an incredible personal production and has an incredibly powerful team that includes family. And it works! Marty has been selling residential real estate in Southern California for Century 21 for the past 36 years. She has an incredible real estate sales record, both in the Nation and in the WORLD. Marty and her team have sold over a Billion Dollars in real estate. I know you will enjoy meeting her and find her just as amazing as I do!

Debbie: **Marty how old were you when you got into the business?**

Marty: I was 27 and had two small kids. I decided to partner with another lady in my office due to my demanding home life and that worked for about 5 years..

At the end of the first 5 years the kids were a bit older and I found I was much more aggressive than my partner and knew it was time to move on. So I gave her all the farm areas and stepped away and started fresh.

I immediately hired a housekeeper. My husband didn't want me to spend the money until he saw how much my production increased and then he was 100% behind me and told me, "Don't make another bed ever. Just go sell something!"

Debbie: **Marty, I believe you got into the business in 1978 so you have lived through many market cycles haven't you?**

Marty: Yes, Debbie it has been a wild and crazy ride. In the early 80's fixed rates were 18% and then again in 1989 the market turned and I had to work hard to get properties sold. I had to spend more on marketing. And then in '98 the market took another dive. Throughout all of this though I got my properties sold and became known as the person who could get the job done no matter what!

People have called me the Wayne Gretzky because I can sell anything and I have the ability to read the market, see what's coming, and quickly adjust. This allows me to help my clients take advantage of opportunities and maximize their profits.

Debbie: **Marty, you have always maintained a very high personal production. What were your numbers in your best year?**

Marty: 224 closed units by myself. Now, while my numbers are high, my team also creates some great production, much of that though is fueled by the leads I generate with my aggressive marketing and prospecting.

I am the head rainmaker and the closer that steps in when they need me to put a deal together.

People always ask me how I did it when there were no computers, cell phones, and DocuSign, I tell them I prospected, prospected,

prospected! And I still do.

Debbie: **What do you do to stay current and ahead of the competition?**

Marty: We had to adjust to technology and keeping up with the times and next generation tools and techniques and I keep young people around me. My kids work with me and help me stay ahead of the curve.

Debbie: **What makes your team successful?**

Marty: I am not greedy and I take good care of them and give good leads and help them close them. I value and appreciate them and they know it.

My goal is to put the right people in place to maximize talents and I try to match the personalities of the clients with the right agent on the team so that everyone is happy.

I admit I am tough on them, I want them to win and I don't back down. We set strong goals and I hold the team accountable.

They love me and they fear me a little because they know I have really high standards. We need to respect the customers and their dependency on us and be committed to an exceptional level of service. I won't tolerate anything less than excellent. My advice to new people- prospect like a maniac, set a budget, and have a game plan. Everywhere you go you prospect, don't be a secret agent. There are leads everywhere. Stop waiting for them to find you and go get them.

Boris Kholodov
Toronto, ON
Phone: (416) 920-2220
Email: boris@agentboris.com

Over the past thirteen years Boris has successfully completed over 1,000 transactions.. His career highlights include achieving multiple record price sales, including top prices per square foot ever reached in several top-tier condominium buildings, the second highest price ever achieved for a freehold townhouse, and the top price ever paid per square foot (gross floor area) for a single family home.

Debbie: **What attracted you to real estate?**

Boris: The image of the successful real estate agent in his expensive car enjoying his flexible schedule, meeting interesting clients, and receiving a stack of commission checks attracted me very much when I was an innocent 18-year-old political science student. It seemed so easy: people just call you, you show them a couple of nice houses, they buy one, you get paid, they love you and send you their friends.... I decided to do it part time while I was still in school. What was I thinking?!!!

Debbie: **Why do you feel you have been so successful when so many others have failed?**

Boris: After I obtained my license, I realized that the profession was a hundred times less sexy and a thousand times more difficult than I had thought. But I was young, naïve, hungry, and determined so I never gave up. I made success my only choice.

Debbie: **What is unique about you, the services you bring to your clients, and how you attract business?**

Boris: To obtain new business I play the numbers game. I market my services consistently to thousands of people in my target market. Once new prospects call, I convert them into clients by showing them that I have the power to tilt the outcome in their favor. My most loyal clients value me not just as a salesperson, but also as a creative strategist, a marketer, and a negotiator. They know that it pays to have me on their side.

Debbie: **If you were entering the business today what would you do differently?**

Boris: In my early years, I regret not having kept in touch with some of my past clients, leaving them for the competition to snap up. I learned that if you forget your clients, they will forget you.

Debbie: **What would be your advice to new agents that would help them succeed?**

Boris: To succeed as a salesperson, you don't have to re-invent the wheel. Stick to the basics. Clients love simplicity. Let the competition confuse them and then come and make it simple for them. They will love you.

Debbie: **What do you love about what you do?**

Boris: I love the chase. Chasing the coveted listing, chasing the deal, chasing a ridiculously high production goal – this makes me feel alive and successful.

Debbie: **What are some of your biggest challenges?**

Boris: When I was single, I devoted my entire life to the business. Now, as a father of two, I am struggling to achieve a healthy work-family balance. So far, I have only figured out one way: be more efficient and waste no time. I used to go on many unproductive appointments and now I am significantly more selective on how I invest time. When I go on that late-night appointment and leave my family behind, I have to make it worth it!

Debbie: **What is your goal for the year 2014?**

Boris: I am a procrastinator at heart and am notorious for showing up late (usually by about 10 minutes) to meetings and appointments. This year, my goal is to be always on time.

Don De Grote
Seal Beach, CA
Phone: (562) 598-6970
Email: don@degrote.com

Don has been in the Real Estate business for 32 years, is in the top 1% of realtors nationwide, and has been a First Team Hall of Fame Award Winner for 19 years. In addition to his vast experience in residential real estate Don is also an approved relocation specialist, senior residential specialist, and probate and trust specialist.

Furthermore, Don manages various investments and rental properties as well as acting as Chief Operating Officer of Excelleum Coaching & Consulting.

Debbie: **Don, as most of the readers know by now you are my husband and have been in the business for 32+ years.**

You have had the opportunity to watch me do a crazy amount of deals, and you chose instead to build a very solid and productive career that centers around a geographic farm and a database with

minimal stress and chaos. **Maybe you can share your thoughts on having a narrow focus on where your business comes from.**

Don: In the early years I did all the various types of prospecting, and that was great for ramping up my career. When you left active sales to become a coach I was left with your database along with my own to manage.

I decided that if I focused on being in constant communication with my clients and delivering white glove service I could really build a business that I could enjoy and that would serve me well for many years to come.

It's the same reason I decided to be a geographic farmer because I like warm prospecting. While it takes some time to win over the people in the farm- once you do farming becomes very profitable and very simple.

I do, of course, make sales from other sources. In fact, many agents refer clients to me because they are confident I will get the deal done and get them paid.

Debbie: **Can you tell them a little bit about what you do to connect with these groups?**

Don: I do what you talk about in the book actually. I call them regularly- this process is calendared and systematic so I'm sure not to miss anyone. I also call them on their birthdays and I call the AAA's even more often.

I hard copy mail to them monthly and email them with important updates and information.

But most importantly I do deliver A+ service. In all the years in business I have never been sued, and clients don't complain, they rave about us. That makes me happy!

My geographic farms receive at least 2 pieces a month, and I knock the doors periodically throughout the year. I used to knock the farm monthly, up until this past year and now I'm working with a new strategy, mixing up calling them with knocking to reach different people at different times.

Debbie: **Of course, since we built the systems together I know that everything you do is set up and calendared so that you never miss a beat. Many people reading this book might be working with a spouse, a partner or a family member. You have done all of the above, any advice for them in terms of how to make it all work?**

Don: I think the most important thing is that each person has to be honest about their strengths and talents and stay in their zone. Debbie, you used to love holding open houses and were great at converting buyers from it. I don't like open house and I no longer want to go after cold prospects, so I simply focus on what I do like but I make sure to really dig in and squeeze all the opportunity from it.

Working with family can be challenging and yet, also very rewarding. With Erika our daughter joining me in the business it gives me a chance to pass on all that I have learned and I get to spend more time with her.

Debbie: **Don, your production consistently ranks you in the top in your office and marketplace, however you have never aspired to have a big team and go after the huge numbers. Can you tell the readers why that is?**

Don: Simple, I have to put up with you and as everyone can probably imagine you create a lot of projects! Also we have multiple businesses running, the investments, the real estate sales, and then some of the operational and financial pieces of the coaching business I manage. So I wear a lot of hats by having management duties in each of the businesses we operate and that consumes a lot of my time.

I have never thought I would enjoy managing a large team, what I do enjoy though is mentoring and building young talent. In the last year Chad Engle joined me as a junior associate. He is doing well and while I do not count his production as part of my own I do have an opportunity to earn additional revenue from his efforts. And I have the reward of helping him close deals he wouldn't be able to close on his own.

With our daughter Erika now also working with us in the business that has inspired me to do even more to build the business to provide a bright future for she and Chad. I may add even one more additional protégé this year.

I believe in having the young talent because it is a way to give back and help them grow and it keeps me current with the tools and next generation technologies, and it's fun.

I am also looking forward to coaching a small select group of clients for Excelleum as well.

Debbie: **As Erika joins you in the business what are you telling her?**

Don: Work hard! Prospect constantly and be gracious to everyone. I am stressing that it's a profitable business but not an easy business and she needs to be realistic about what it will take to be a top producer.

We also work on the meaning of customer service. I am constantly reminding her to be gracious and respectful to everyone, vendors, other agents, and of course our clients, even those who are difficult.

Agents and vendors in our market go out of their way to work with me and I want her to have that same quality of reputation. Erika knows too that the training never stops and that she always needs to be striving to learn new things and fortunately she has a great coach, her mom!

I do feel there is opportunity in this business and it has been terrific for our family, however it's not glamorous and certainly not always fun. It's a job and you don't have to love it every day to do it well. If you did, that would be called vacation!